You'd Fly Laughing Too

by Garth Wallace

Published by
Happy Landings

Other books by Garth Wallace

Fly Yellow Side Up
Pie In The Sky
Derry Air
Cockpit Follies
The Flying Circus
If Clouds Could Talk
Don't Call Me a Legend
Blue Collar Pilots

National Library of Canada Cataloguing in Publication

You'd Fly Laughing Too
fiction, humour, aviation

Written by: Garth Wallace

ISBN 0-9739214-0-4

I. Title.

PS8595.A56516I5 2003 C813'.54 C2003-905242-7

Cover and inside artwork: Francois Bougie, Bizzart

Editing: Liz Wallace, Sari Funston & Francois Bougie

Layout and typesetting: Happy Landings

Written, illustrated, typeset, printed and bound in Canada

Published October, 2005

Published by:

Happy Landings
851 Heritage Dr. RR #4
Merrickville, Ontario
Canada K0G 1N0
Tel.: 613-269-2552
Fax: 613-269-3962
E-mail: books@happylandings.com
Web site: www.happylandings.com

You'd Fly Laughing Too

Contents

It is permissible to laugh out loud when reading this book.

Introduction

You'd Fly Laughing Too is fiction but real small town aviation is just as exciting, challenging, rewarding and fun.

Garth Wallace
October, 2005

Dedication

You'd Fly Laughing Too is dedicated to all friends, relatives and acquaintances of aviators. Thank you for sharing in your aviators' infectious good nature, frequent laughter, permanent sense of adventure and amazing resistance to stress.

If you are struggling with an aviator's good nature, there is an antidote. Read this book. You'll be sampling why aviators have so much fun and you'll be laughing too.

Garth Wallace

Happy Landings Publishing

Our readers laugh

Chapter One

Dreamers and doers

My mind becomes a loose cannon in bad weather. Sound reasoning takes a holiday and shaky ideas mushroom into grand schemes when I can't fly.

This time I was shivering inside the flying school's portable office, manning the phone and sipping bad coffee. A late winter blizzard had forced the cancellation of our flying. Blowing snow whipped past the windows and a small drift advanced across the floor from under the door.

Henry Rains, my flying school partner, was in the hangar installing a turn coordinator instrument in an airplane. I was the one in the office because Henry loved the winter and he knew how to do mechanical stuff. I didn't. Henry was from Saskatchewan where cold isn't cold until exposed flesh freezes in 20 seconds. My partner was working in the unheated hangar enjoying what he considered a zero degree Fahrenheit winter heat wave.

I picked up an aviation newspaper in my gloved hands and scanned the classifieds. An advertisement caught my eye:

> For sale - Banner towing equipment:
> 250 large letters, 3 lead masts, 2 tails,
> connectors. Asking $1,500. Call Tex.

I had seen small airplanes chugging over the beaches of Florida towing advertisements. My mind clicked into gear. Maybe it would work here.

"Here" was the City of Circus. Henry and I operated The Flying Circus, a small flight training and aircraft charter business. The Circus Airport was not far from Niagara Falls, one of the most popular natural tourist attractions in the world. The Falls was surrounded by a neon jungle of restaurants, motels and souvenir shops competing for tourist dollars. Aerial advertising would be a sure moneymaker, I thought to myself. I read the newspaper ad again. According to the area code, the seller was nearby.

Balanced against my enthusiasm for questionable projects were my partner and his wife. A year earlier, Henry Rains and I had been two overworked, underpaid flying instructors with a dream of starting our own air service. The dream turned to reality when we leased four airplanes and borrowed money to build a hangar and buy an office. Now we were living the dream. We were two overworked, underpaid flying instructors with our own small company and a large debt.

Henry was the solid half of the partnership. He was tall, fair-haired and calm. His prairie heritage had left him with an innocent-looking face and an active mind. That we were still in business was a credit to my partner's stubborn practicality. Henry lived by one simple rule: if it doesn't make sense, don't do it. It worked annoyingly well.

Henry's wife was also a major factor in our survival. Leanne Rains was our receptionist, bookkeeper, office manager, mother confessor and do-everything-else person. She landed the job by default. We needed her and she was available.

The mother-of-two juggled our start-up debt and operating costs against an income that was earned by the hour only in good weather. Leanne had a genuine, welcoming interest in people that she put to good use. Customers gladly paid for a block of lessons in advance and thanked her for suggesting it. She cheerfully chatted up our suppliers while mentioning that a reduced portion of our shrinking winter income would be sent as payment that week.

I was the dreamer. I invented the advertising and promotion ideas. We worked well together. If the other two liked one of my suggestions, they made it fly. I was also a full-time pilot and flying instructor. Right now we needed more flyable weather and fewer ideas. We were facing the possibility of losing what we had worked so hard to establish if our income didn't improve.

My chilled brain was trying to fit the purchase and operation of banner towing equipment into the realities of our small business when Henry opened the door to the office.

"I'm looking forward to the day we can afford a door on the hangar," he said, stomping his feet.

"I thought you liked this weather."

"I do but it's hard to fix an airplane that's filling with snow."

Henry was also a pilot. He saved us money by working on the airplanes on days like this. He was not a certified mechanic, just a practical country boy who knew how to keep things running. He theorized that if he fixed something, then it wasn't broken so it didn't need an inspection and signature from an aircraft engineer. The regular maintenance and inspections of our fleet were contracted out to an operation at the Derry Airport about 20 minutes flying time away.

He flashed me a grin, "Who's idea was it to face the hangar opening to the north?"

"Mine," I replied, "I didn't want the rest of the airport to see you fixing airplanes."

His grin widened, "If I don't know what I'm doing, how would they?"

He unzipped his parka and stepped out of his fleece-lined boots.

"I'd rather they thought you were doing illegal maintenance," I joked, "than witness that you are."

Henry walked over to the coffeepot and filled a cup. He sat down with his coat open. He sipped on the coffee, winced and sipped some more. "Boy, you make the world's worst coffee."

"Leanne made that pot," I replied. "I just warmed it up."

"You mean this is yesterday's coffee?"

I smiled and nodded.

"I must have the world's cheapest partner."

"Right now, that's who you need."

"I suppose," he grumbled.

"Speaking of business," I said, "what do you think of towing advertising banners over Niagara Falls this summer for additional revenue?"

He sipped more coffee and looked at me over the rim of his cup. "I thought you might be in here cooking something up. I came in to see what it was this time."

I showed him the ad in the newspaper. He read it, twice.

"Of course, it makes perfect sense," he said. "We know nothing about advertising; we have never towed anything with an airplane; we have no experience with the banner equipment; and we have no money or credit."

I smiled. "You're right but what's the show stopper?"

"What airplane would we use?"

"We could rig all four with release hooks and use whatever is available."

Henry pondered that one for a moment. "Who teaches us how

to do it?"

"The guy selling the equipment."

He nodded his head up and down and said, "It might be worth checking into."

"You think so?" It wasn't the response that I was expecting.

"Sure. Either you've figured out how to overcome the reasons not to or you never will. All I have to do is listen and nod my head. Did you call this guy?"

"No."

Henry handed me the newspaper. "Give him a ring," he grinned. "Today is a good time. We're on the ground and our bookkeeper isn't here."

I called the phone number. Tex answered. He sounded like a man who thought slowly and talked slower.

He said that the letters were used but not by him. "I was going to tow 'em with my Stinson L-5 but it's costing me too much to fix 'er up."

Tex told me that his letters were the large ones. Each was seven feet high and three feet wide, big enough to be read at 1,000 feet.

"So they're the right size for towing over Niagara Falls," I said.

"Well, that depends on the kinda airplane you got," he replied in his raspy voice.

"Piper Cherokee 140 and Cessna 172."

"You kin only pull 'bout ten of these 'ere letters with a Cherokee," he wheezed.

"So we need a more powerful airplane?"

"Yup, or an advertising feller who don't wanna say much."

"OK, thank you anyway," I said.

I related the other side of the conversation to Henry.

"We can't afford a more powerful airplane," I concluded. "Forget I mentioned the banner towing."

"Hey, it only cost us a phone call. I like those ideas."

Chapter Two

Things go better with Hitchcock

"Can we tow advertising banners with this airplane?" Don Hitchcock asked me from the back seat.

I partially turned my head to reply. "It's funny you'd mention it. Henry and I looked into that just last week. Why do you ask?"

"We're calling an election this spring," the politician replied. "I thought we'd advertise for my re-election with the airplane. Heck," he chuckled, "we could tow banners on these trips around the lake. Look at those commuters stuck in their cars down there with nothing to do but read about me."

My passenger was The Honourable Donald Hitchcock, a cabinet minister in the provincial legislature. We were flying in his two-seat Champion Citabria. It was a cool but clear Friday afternoon in early March. We were homebound from Toronto's downtown airport, scooting along the Lake Ontario shoreline.

"I can see the banners now," Don giggled in the back seat. "'GO HIGHER WITH HITCHCOCK', or how about, 'PUT A LITTLE MOONSHINE IN YOUR LIFE, VOTE HITCHCOCK'."

Don was a happy guy on the far side of middle age. His hair was thinning, his girth was widening but his smile was constant. Don's Citabria was an aerobatic training airplane. The fun-loving politician had purchased it to commute weekly from his home in Niagara Falls to Toronto, the provincial capital. I was Don's "corporate" pilot. It was my job to spice up the 40-minute flights with loops and rolls when asked. I taught aerobatics with the little high-wing airplane at The Flying Circus when I wasn't chauffeuring Don.

"Can we tow a banner that says, 'VOTE FOR HITCHCOCK' right side up and then, 'VOTE FOR HITCHCOCK' upside down?

We could fly home doing a series of rolls."

"I'm afraid not, Don. We found out that the Citabria is not powerful enough to tow the banner size we would need."

"Darn. Maybe I should get a bigger plane," he mused. "A Lear Jet could tow all sorts of lies about me."

"We need something slow and powerful," I replied, "like a Stearman or a Beaver."

"A Stearman has an open cockpit, right? I don't want to lose any more hair. We could mount floats on a Beaver and commute across the lake to Toronto Harbour each week. You could teach float flying back at Circus and we could go fishing on weekends."

I smiled to myself. Don was in the right job. He loved to talk.

"You're not a fisherman, Don."

"I know, but I could be. A sport that includes weekends out of the house, alcohol and swapping lies with friends can't be all bad." Don laughed at his own joke. "Speaking of alcohol..."

The back seat went quiet. The smell of bourbon told me that Don was helping himself to the refreshment that was stowed under my seat. Between sips, he called out campaign slogans.

"'DON'T WORRY BE HAPPY VOTE HITCHCOCK.'" That one made him chuckle.

"'TAXES HIGH? VOTE HITCHCOCK AND SEE WHY!' I guess that one won't fly," he said. "How about, 'HITCHCOCK, GOOD TO THE LAST DROP.'"

Don telephoned me during the following week. He sounded excited.

"How many letters will a Super Cub tow?"

"Not as many as a Beaver," I replied.

"I know, I know, but will it pull enough?"

"Hang on."

"I'm hanging," he snickered.

I had ordered a banner towing manual and had skimmed through it once. I reached for it behind the flight desk and flipped to a chart.

"It says a maximum of 35 seven-foot characters for a Super Cub."

"Hot diggity!" Don whooped. "That's perfect, isn't it?"

"Well, Don, a Beaver will pull 50 along with a canoe strapped to the side and a cabin full of beer, but 35 is a good-sized ad."

"I don't drink beer and you'll never catch me in a canoe," he declared, "so Super Cub it is!"

"Ah... Don," I sputtered, "hold on. Before you go airplane

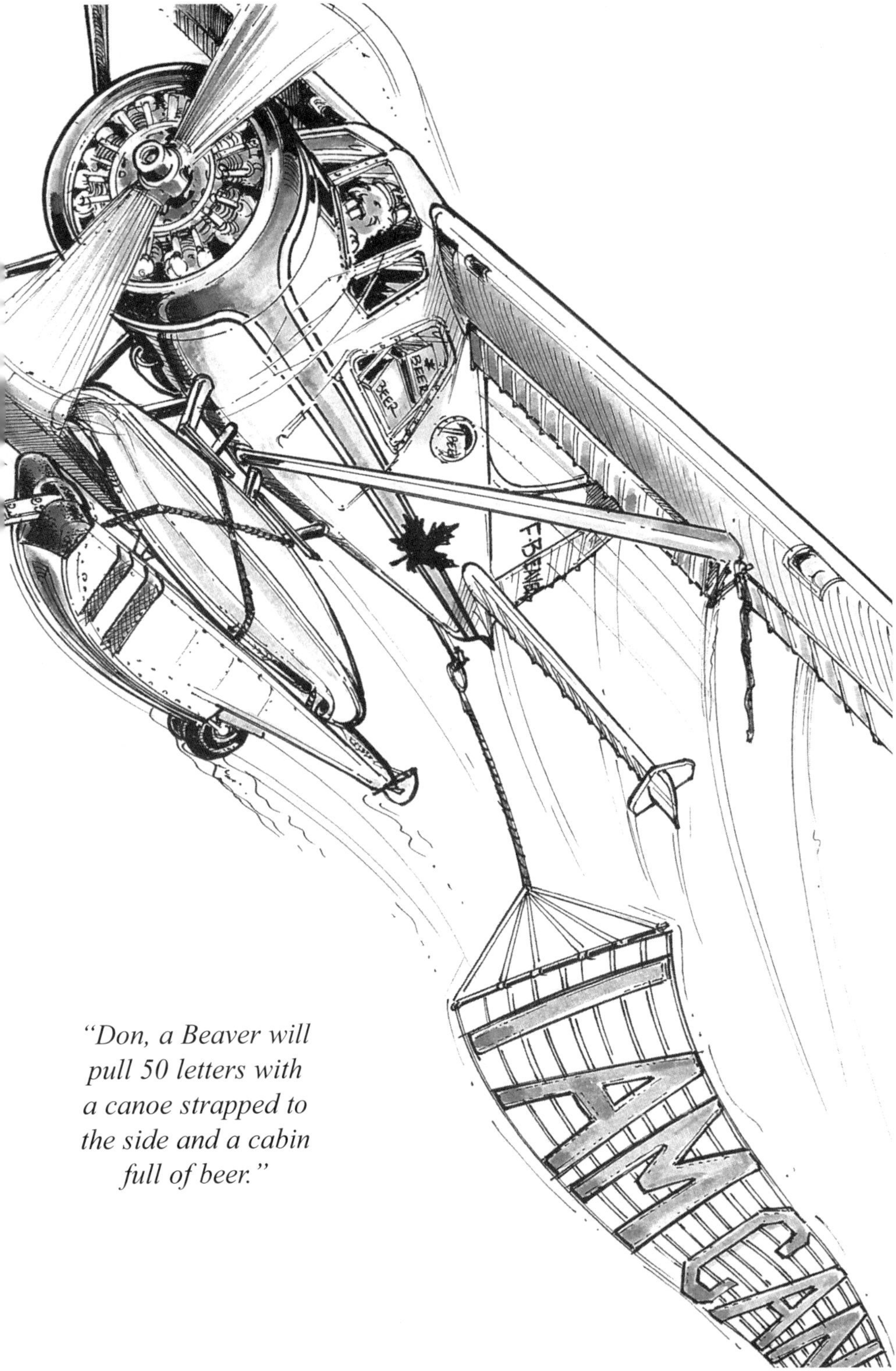

"Don, a Beaver will pull 50 letters with a canoe strapped to the side and a cabin full of beer."

shopping, let us help you this time."

Don had purchased his Citabria from Skid Sicamore, an aviation low-life who worked out of the trunk of his car. The deal had turned out OK but it had been pure luck.

"Oh, I haven't forgotten," Don replied. "You can sell the Citabria for me. We've got three weeks before the Cub is delivered. The Citabria money will pay the balance."

"Ah, Don, you're losing me. What Cub? What balance?"

"I put a deposit on a new Super Cub yesterday. Did you know that Piper is phasing out their Cub production? I bought one of the last delivery positions available. Neat eh?"

That was irrepressible Don. His mind easily bounced from a 450-horsepower, seven-place Beaver on floats to a 150-hp, two-place Super Cub.

"We can't tow those letters with the Cub on floats, Don."

"Oh, I forgot about the floats. That's OK. We don't want to tow them over water, anyway. Fish can't read and they don't vote.

The projected delivery date for the new airplane was April 1st. The timing was perfect for banner towing. Don's political campaign was set to launch mid-April and so was the Niagara Falls summer tourist season.

"April 1st is a Saturday this year," I said to Henry, after telling him about Don's purchase.

We were in one of our end-of-the-day "business meetings" in the open hangar. I was cleaning scum off the aircraft leading edges with a bucket of dish soap and hot water. Henry was adding oil to the engines.

"How about having a barbeque/open house to introduce the new aircraft?"

"An open house is a good idea," my partner replied, "but April 1st might be tight. The delivery date on the Cub will slip. They usually do."

"Then we'll call it 'The Flying Circus April Fools' Barbeque and Open House'. We'll have other activities so people will come even if there is no new airplane."

Henry gave me a "like what?" look.

My mind was running with the idea. "We could promote the arrival of a new business jet as an April Fool's joke."

"These are customers, not family. You may get a bad reaction when they come out to the airport and find no jet."

"We'll have a barbeque, display aircraft for sale, draw for door prizes and stage a spot landing competition," I said, warming my hands in the wash bucket.

"It sounds like you have it all figured out," Henry said. He tipped an oil jug into the engine of a Cherokee.

"I'm just getting started."

"Then I won't waste time trying to talk you out of it."

I called Al Milton the next day. Al was a customer who had helped us with a barbeque last year. Al was a party lover who owned a large portable grill. He was also a government meat inspector with a freezer full of confiscated product. I arranged with him to bring his barbeque and grilling steaks on April 1.

Then I spoke to Barney Swallow about dusting temporary lines across the active runway for the spot landing contest. Barney was the antique who managed the Circus Airport for the city.

"You have to include the flying club," the old warrior had rasped, "if you're going to tie up traffic with some fool contest."

"Yes sir, I'll invite the club; the more the merrier."

The Circus Flying Club was our competition across the ramp.

"Can you join us at the open house?" I asked.

"Is it on a weekend?"

"Saturday, April 1st."

"You can count on me. I won't be there."

Leanne and I made up a Flying Circus customer newsletter and mailed it mid-March:

The Flying Circus Flyer

April Fools' Barbeque/Open House

Date: Saturday, April 1
Time: 10:00 to 15:00
Barbeque: All proceeds donated to charity.
steaks - $2, steak plates - $2, steak buns - $2
tubesteaks - $1, tubesteak buns - $1
pop - $1, coffee - $.50 coffee cups - $.50

Display of aircraft for sale

Spot Landing Contest

A precision landing contest will run during the Barbeque/Open House.
Rental pilots, aircraft owners and student pilots are welcome to join the fun.
The entry fee will be $10 for three attempts.
The pilot landing closest to the spot will receive *The Flying Circus Spot Landing Trophy.*
Pilots who need coaching and practise are welcome to book dual and solo time before the contest.

Our April 1st Special Guest:

Challenger 601

Meet the latest addition to The Flying Circus fleet.
April 1 is the projected delivery date for our first all-new aircraft, a Canadair Challenger 601.
The wide-bodied, pressurized, business jet will be a welcome boost to our charter department.
The airplane will be available for dual instruction at $ 9,981.50 per hour.
A big thank you to the government's new *Make Debt Financing Program for Small Business*. Normally the $20-million price for the Challenger would be out of our league but with zero down, zero interest and principal payments tied to the flying time only, we were able to swing it.
So come and help us celebrate this bold new acquisition. Look for the executive jet painted all red (to match the ink in our books).
The registration letters are: **A-FOOL.**

Chapter Three

It's Melville

"Did you see that you're scheduled with Melville on Friday?" Leanne Rains asked.

I was checking the booking sheets on the flight desk. I flipped the pages to the end of the week.

"OK."

"It's for a spring checkout," she added.

I smiled. "So he's flying his airplane here from the farm so I can check out his flying?"

"Apparently," our receptionist answered. "It gets better. When he's done here, he's flying to Derry to have Darcy Philips do the annual inspection on the airplane."

I laughed. "It's his farmer logic. If he doesn't survive the flight here, he saves the cost of the checkout. If the airplane doesn't make it to Derry, he won't have to pay for an inspection."

"You understand, but is it smart?"

"It's Melville."

I had taught Melville Passmore to fly a few years ago. He was stubby, slightly grubby but always friendly. The likeable country boy lived and worked with his parents on their farm south of the City of Derry.

Melville had been struggling to learn how to fly when I met him. He had 63 hours in the air but had never flown solo. I was his eighteenth instructor. As we flew together, I gradually realized that the problem was the teaching, not the learning. The young farmer absorbed knowledge from life rather than from books or instruction. I discovered that Melville knew more about machinery than many mechanics. He could predict weather by looking at the sky and he had developed his own visual form of mathematics. He kept track of the winter feed on the farm by comparing the size of the herd to the size of the hay stacked in the mow rather than by the number of cows and bales.

Once I woke up to this, Melville struggled less and eventually earned a Private Pilot Licence. He bought a 1959 Piper TriPacer and kept it in a shed beside the landing strip on the family homestead.

Friday arrived and so did Melville. I was making coffee when his voice boomed over our office radio.

"Circus Tower... this is TriPacer Charlie Lima Oscar Whiskey November... over."

The Circus air traffic controllers were familiar with Melville's loud, halting, radio voice. He transmitted like he was calling the cows home.

"Hi there Melville, long time no hear," the controller replied. "You are cleared... I mean, Lima Oscar Whiskey November is cleared to join a left downwind for Runway 24, wind 240, 10 to 15, altimeter 30.01. I have no other traffic at this time. Call joining the circuit."

There was a long pause. I could picture Melville waiting to be sure the controller was done, then licking his lips, pulling in his tongue, pushing the microphone button and hollering, "Roger... Lima Oscar Whiskey November."

There was never doubt which airplane was Melville's. A previous owner had painted the TriPacer in orange and black stripes. It looked like a sunburned zebra. The colourful airplane joined the circuit and landed on Runway 24. I watched Melville taxi onto our ramp and then I walked outside to greet him.

The right side door burst open on the TriPacer. Melville charged from the airplane like a bull out of the barn in spring.

"I'm getting married!" he shouted. "I'm getting married!" He galloped across the tarmac toward me.

I held out my hand as a greeting and mirrored some of his enthusiasm. "Hey, congratulations!"

"I'm getting married!" he declared once more.

He stopped before crashing into me, grabbed my hand with both of his and pumped it up and down like a floor jack.

"Who's the lucky lady?" I asked.

"The girl I met in church."

"The one you took flying?"

"Yes!"

I remembered the girl. She was shy, pretty in a wholesome way and dressed nicely in clothes that seemed to be two generations past.

"Wow, that girl was a knock-out. Won't your cows be jealous?"

Melville was so excited, he missed my humour. He puffed out his

He grabbed my hand and pumped it up and down like a floor jack.

chest and said, "She's going to be Mrs. Mary Ellen Passmore!"

"She's a lucky girl," I declared. The farm boy was not the best smelling bachelor in the world but I kept that thought to myself.

"I want you to be my best man!" Melville announced loudly.

The request caught me off guard. My brain flashed to a picture of me standing by the altar in a church full of Melville's stubby relatives dressed in coveralls and rubber boots.

"Well, Melville, I appreciate being asked," I replied slowly. I was scrambling for a reason to decline. "You must have a family member or a friend who knows you better."

He shook his head from side to side. "Nope. I've spent more time with you in the past three years than anyone 'cept the cows. You hafta be my best man."

I couldn't dispute our time together and I couldn't think of another way of saying, No.

"Well, if you're sure, Melville, I'd be honoured to be your best man."

He threw his arms into the air and shouted. "Yahoo! I can't wait to tell Mary Ellen!"

"Give her my best," I said. "In the meantime, Romeo, are we going flying?"

"Yes! I wanna learn those spot landings for the contest."

"All right, Master Passmore the betrothed, let's go into the office first."

Melville led the way. Inside, he announced his upcoming marriage. Leanne returned his excitement and gave him a motherly hug.

"When's the big day?" she asked.

"Two weeks," he declared. "Saturday, April 1st!"

Oh no, I said to myself. Now what do I do?

I waited until the lover boy had made the rounds of everyone in the room. Then I sat him down.

"We'll do a short briefing on spot landings, Melville, but first, we have a problem with your wedding being so soon. It's on the same day as the open house and landing contest."

"Yeah, I know," he answered right away. "Mary Ellen didn't want the date announced until the marriage banns had been read in the church. That ends this Sunday. April is planting time, so the latest date had to be April 1st."

"Getting married is a big event. Maybe you should skip flying here and concentrate on the wedding."

Melville shook his head back and forth. "No way. The women don't want me around." He furrowed his brow in concentration, placed his left elbow on the table, held up his hand and bent each finger down as he explained. "First, the open house ends at three o'clock. Second, the wedding ceremony starts at four-thirty. I can fly us to my place. Third, we change clothes and drive to the church. Fourth, the ceremony and good wishes last an hour, then everyone goes home for milking. Fifth, we meet again at the community hall for the reception supper at seven."

"What happens if we're held up along the way?"

His face split into a grin. "You're my best man! You'll make sure I get to the church on time!"

Chapter Four

On the edge

"What speed do you fly on approach to the farm?" I was briefing Melville on spot landings. The Passmore's grass runway was short and had obstacles at both ends.

"Seventy-five? That's what you taught me, isn't it?"

"Yes. How much flap?"

"Full flap?"

"Correct. And what power do you carry into the flare-out?"

"Is this a trick question?"

"Yes."

"None?"

"That's right but what if you need power?"

"I go around?"

"Very good."

"Can we go flying now?"

"Soon. So you set up a power-off glide at 75 miles per hour with full flap. Then what?"

"I land?"

"Yes, but where do you touch down?"

He frowned, "On the runway?"

"Right, but how far down the runway?"

His frown deepened, "Which runway?"

"Do you land on the same spot each time?"

"No?"

"You don't?" I was surprised. The Passmore strip was short. The farmer pilot would need to nail the same spot to have room to stop.

Melville looked around and then at the floor. Questions made him nervous. The fear came from years at school where he couldn't answer most of them.

"If not on the same spot, where do you land?"

"If I'm landing over the wires, I touch down a quarter of the way from the wires or I go around. If I'm approaching the other way, I land a quarter length from the trees."

It was an example of Melville learning things his way.

I smiled. "So you land the same distance from the beginning of the runway approaching from either way."

"If you say so."

"I do, trust me. That means you already know how to spot land your airplane anywhere."

Melville scratched his head. "How do I know that?"

"Just apply the technique you use at home. In the spot landing contest here, picture your grass strip on top of the active runway and land like you were at the farm."

Melville looked puzzled. His eyes started glazing over. His mind was slipping into neutral.

"Come on," I said, "we'll go flying and I'll show you."

Melville and his airplane were a good match. The TriPacer had short fat wings, a stubby fuselage and stocky legs. It resembled a milking stool from a distance. It flew like a milking stool too but Melville loved his plane. He found it easy to handle once he mastered its stubby flying habits.

The two of us squeezed into the TriPacer's front seat. Melville started the engine and called the control tower for taxi instructions. A light wind was blowing from the southwest. We were given Runway 24. It was the airport's largest runway at 150 feet wide and 5,000 feet long. It would be a good test of myspot landing teaching method.

"Do a normal takeoff, Melville," I said. We were beside the runway and ready to go. "Then come around and approach like you were landing at your home strip."

Melville's tongue was hanging out one side of his mouth. It's where he parked it when he was concentrating. He licked his lips, pulled in the tongue, took a deep breath and punched the microphone button, "Lima Oscar Whiskey November, ready to takeoff Runway 24 for circuits." His voice boomed like a circus ringmaster.

"Zebra One is cleared for takeoff Runway 24," the controller joked, "wind 240 at five. Call on the downwind."

Melville grinned. He liked the kidding but he never returned it on the radio. It was too much like public speaking. He replied by the book. "Lima Oscar Whiskey November, roger."

The young farmer added power and taxied onto the runway.

Melville flew his airplane like he did everything else: with animation and commentary. He took off and climbed the TriPacer in the standard circuit pattern. His body moved constantly. He leaned forward to look for traffic and then sat back to stab a finger at a gauge that he was checking.

His lips moved too. "One thousand feet," he announced loudly, "nose level, power twenty-two hundred rpm, check for traffic, turn downwind."

I had taught Melville to fly in Piper Cherokee 140s. They were roomy enough that I could shrink against the door to avoid his gyrations. There was less room in the TriPacer. I was nudged, bumped and bruised as he thrust a finger at each instrument and touched each control on the pre-landing checklist.

"Ask the tower for a stop and go, Melville."

He did.

"Oscar Whiskey November is cleared stop and go Runway 24," the controller replied, "wind 230 at six."

"Oscar Whiskey November, roger."

Melville continued issuing instructions to himself. "Check for traffic, turn base, reduce power, nose level, flaps down, 75 mph, nose down."

TriPacers are ideal airplanes for spot landings. The pilot just has to fly a power-on approach until the landing spot disappears under the airplane's nose and then cut the power to idle. The short-winged airplane drops onto the spot like a fireman down a pole.

I pointed ahead as Melville turned us onto the final approach. "Picture a row of trees at the beginning of this runway."

Melville leaned forward. "Trees at the beginning of the runway," he repeated.

"Right. Now visualize your landing strip in front of you instead of this runway."

Melville furrowed his brow. "I don't see it."

We were half a mile from touchdown.

"You won't see it," I replied quickly, "picture it in your head and land the airplane like you were at home."

"OK." Melville sucked in a deep breath and cut the engine power. "Picture the strip at home," he said to himself.

The TriPacer dropped like a stone. I could see we were going to land short of the runway. I looked at Melville. His eyes were shut tight.

"I think I got it," he declared.

I wanted the young farmer to see his mistake and correct it but I did not want to wreck his airplane.

"Good, have a look."

Melville opened one eye and peered ahead. The grass in front of the runway was rushing up to meet us. His other eye popped open.

"I have control!" I barked. I applied full power and raised the nose.

The descent slowed, the airplane hovered over the ground and then it struggled into a climb.

Melville looked at me as if he had done something wrong. He had but it had been my fault. I hadn't counted on his closing his eyes. I needed to find an approach that worked for him.

"You have control," I said. "We'll try something different. Take us around for another circuit."

On the next downwind leg, I pointed to the runway through Melville's side window. "See the distance markers from the beginning of the runway on each side of the centreline?"

"Yes," he replied cautiously.

"Good. Pretend that the pavement ends at the 2,000-foot mark. Touch down one quarter of the way from the beginning."

Melville visually calculated the spacing using his thumb and forefinger. "OK, I think."

"Call for a stop and go landing and use the same approach that you do at home."

"OK."

"This time don't close your eyes."

Melville nodded. He called the control tower, turned onto the base leg and set up a power-on approach. He shifted forward in his seat to see the runway better. "Two thousand foot mark," he said to himself. He turned left again for the final leg. "Same approach as at home," he said, narrowing his eyes.

Melville cut the power when there was no doubt we could glide to the runway. Down we went. He pulled the control wheel back to land. We were still 50 feet in the air.

The young farmer was being fooled by the wide runway. He was flaring where the size of the big runway fit his smaller grass strip. Now the airplane's energy had been spent and we were too high.

"I have control!" I yelled.

I shoved the throttle in all the way to help ease the TriPacer down. We smacked the asphalt hard enough to bounce us back into the air. I held the nose up, the main wheels hit the runway again and I cut the power. The airplane stayed down. I pulled on the brake lever and stopped.

"What happened?" Melville asked with a surprised look on his face.

"You flared 50 feet above the runway where it looked narrow like it does at home."

We fell silent. Melville looked around while I contemplated what to do next.

He pointed to the right side of the runway. "Can I try a spot landing on the edge of the runway?" he asked tentatively.

"Why do you want to do that?"

We smacked the asphalt hard enough to bounce us back into the air.

Melville blushed and flashed a nervous grin. "That's where I always land at home. The cows like to graze in the clover on the east side of the strip so I always land along the west edge."

"It's worth a try," I shrugged.

The tower controller broke into our conversation. "Do you need assistance Oscar Whiskey November?"

Melville watched me. I nodded. He pressed the microphone button. "No, thank you," he said. He held the transmit button in. I nodded again. "We're ready for another circuit," he announced loudly.

We were cleared to take off. I sat quietly while the determined farm boy leaned forward, hung out his tongue and applied full power. He talked and fidgeted his way around the circuit.

Melville lined up with the right side of the runway on the final approach and cut the power. The trusty Tri-Pacer plummeted. The glide distance looked good but I was ready if we flared too soon. I felt myself leaning left, using body English to keep us out of the grass along the edge. I was elbowed for my trouble.

The TriPacer sailed over the imaginary trees. Melville eased back on the control wheel at the right height. The nose came up and the descent was checked. The main wheels kissed the asphalt about ten feet from the right side. Melville pulled on the brakes and we stopped.

"Perfect!" I declared.

The young pilot beamed.

"Can you do that well along the left side?" I asked.

"Sure. I do that at home when I'm landing the other way."

"Try one here," I said.

The controller called, "Oscar Whiskey November, what are your intentions?"

Melville looked at me. I nodded. He licked his lips, pulled in his tongue and pushed the button. "Lima Oscar Whiskey November requests one more circuit."

"Cleared for takeoff, Oscar Whiskey November, call on the downwind."

"Oscar Whiskey November."

Melville's spot landing on the other side of the runway was perfect.

Back in the office he asked if the contest judges would allow him to land on the edge of the runway.

"Sure, no problem, Melville," I replied with a grin. "Do we have to arrange for cows to be grazing along the other side?"

Melville blushed and grinned, "No, but if you want to, I've got them."

Chapter Five

The Rock

Henry and I bought the banner towing equipment from Tex. Don Hitchcock paid for it. We advertised the Citabria for sale in another issue of The Flying Circus Flyer. The customer newsletter announced that "an exciting new aircraft" would replace it. Henry applied for a government aerial advertising licence and I re-read the Aerial Banner Towing book.

Don called from his office in Toronto two days after the newsletter had been mailed.

"You guys are amazing," the politician declared. "I can't believe you found a buyer so fast."

"Ah... what buyer, Don?" I sputtered. "What are you talking about?"

"The Citabria, it's all but sold. Thanks a lot."

"Ah... Don, wait... What... Who bought the Citabria?"

"You know... What's his name? He says you taught him to fly. He sure is hot-to-trot for that airplane. He'll be there this afternoon to take measurements for floats. The deal doesn't close until the Super Cub arrives. Gotta run."

"Don...?" He had hung up.

I told Henry and Leanne about the call. We speculated on who would walk through our door as the future owner of the Citabria. The three of us discussed whether we could afford to lease it back for aerobatics as well as add the Super Cub to our fleet for banner towing.

"We don't want to lease from just anybody," Leanne warned.

"It's probably one of Don's doctor or lawyer friends," I suggested. "The kind with lots of money but little time and even less flying ability."

"Who is that?" Leanne asked.

"All of them," I laughed.

"But those types don't fly the Citabria," Henry pointed out. "Our aerobatic customers are regular pilots scraping together enough money to live a dream, one hour at a time."

He was right. We still had no idea who might be buying the airplane. We went back to work.

Henry and I were flying when a former student of mine arrived at the office. He asked for me. Leanne chatted him up until I returned.

Rock Headley worked on an assembly line at the local automotive factory. I remembered that Rock was married and had two young kids. His mother had come in and paid for his flying lessons.

"I hope it leads him to a better life," she had said.

Rock had learned quickly. His shift work allowed him to fly almost every day. He earned a Private Pilot Licence in the minimum flying time. I was surprised that he didn't continue his lessons toward a Commercial Pilot Licence. It might have been that he was happy with his life.

Rock's wife never knew where he was. She worked full-time so they could afford day-care for the kids, leaving Rock on the loose. He drove a 1960s red Corvette convertible. He was either cruising the burger stands in the flashy car or he was polishing it.

Rock wore his dark hair slicked back into a duck tail squared off at the bottom. Summer and winter he dressed in a white T-shirt with the short sleeves rolled up to show bicep muscles that went all the way to his ears. A cigarette pack was permanently tucked into one sleeve. I never saw him smoke. The pant legs on his jeans were short enough to show off the silver chains on his black half-Wellington boots.

Rock had once told me that he loved hunting and fishing. He had said he'd do it all the time if his wife could find a better paying job.

All of this was flashing through my mind as Rock grinned and delivered a crushing handshake.

"How ya doing?" he asked. He expertly rolled a toothpick between his lips while he talked.

"Great, Rock," I winced. "How are you?"

Leanne caught my eye. She was dancing behind the flight desk, nodding toward Rock.

"Fine, thank you," Rock replied. "I'd like to see you for a minute when you're done."

"Sure, I'll be right with you."

I debriefed my student and then passed him to Leanne to make another booking.

"What's up, Rock? Are you ready to go after that Commercial Pilot Licence?"

"No, thanks," he smiled, "I'm buying the Citabria."

"Wow! I didn't know you were in the market."

"Well..." he hesitated. He looked around and dropped his voice. "Can we talk in the hangar?"

"Sure."

Rock followed me outside and into the open building. I was a little puzzled by his cloak and dagger manner. He stopped beside the Citabria, rested a foot on top of the right tire and leaned on his knee.

"I've always dreamed of having a plane for flying into the remote fishing spots up north," he explained in a low voice.

"Oh yeah... of course. I should have remembered."

"And I've been working toward that." He looked around to see if anyone was listening. No one was. "I've already set up a base camp near some great fishing lakes."

"Good for you."

"Recently, I picked up a couple of damaged floats that could be made to fit on the Citabria."

"OK, but if you're asking me, the Citabria is only 115 horsepower. I don't think it will perform well on floats."

"Yeah, I thought of that," he said. He straightened up and flexed his arm muscles. "The floats are oversize. One's an EDO 2000 and the other is a CAP 2200. That should help make up for the low power until I find a bigger engine."

"You mean the floats aren't the same?" I exclaimed. "You can't fly it like that!"

"I'll just load extra fuel or gear inside the bigger one and it'll be fine," he replied calmly.

"The government won't let you."

Rock looked around again and then whispered, "The airplane has never been registered on floats. What the government doesn't know won't hurt it."

"You won't get insurance coverage unless the airplane is certified on floats," I countered.

"The only way I can afford the airplane is to skip extras like insurance."

"But insurance will be a loan requirement from your bank."

He smiled and slapped my shoulder, nearly knocking me over.

"Don't worry about it," he said with a forced chuckle, "I struck a deal with Don Hitchcock. I'm giving him and his buddies fishing trips this summer in exchange for some of the purchase price. My mom is covering the rest."

"Rock, the government classifies that as a commercial operation. The non-standard floats and lack of insurance will just be the start of your problems."

"No, no," he replied, shaking his head. "I'm just giving Don a few trips into remote lakes as a friend not a customer so it's no big deal. There won't be much money changing hands."

"Have you at least got a seaplane rating?"

He smiled and looked at the floor. "I've ridden in lots of bushplanes," he replied, "and I can drive a boat."

The more I heard, the less I wanted to know. "Whatever you say, Rock. Why are you telling me all this?"

"Well, I'm glad you asked. I need a favour. I'm going to take measurements from the lower fuselage today to make up struts for the floats. When the deal closes, I'll need your hangar for a day or so to fit the floats on and then fly out of here."

"Who's making your struts?"

He cocked his head and grinned. "The same guy who is going to install them," he replied.

As soon as he said it, I realized that he or an unqualified buddy would do the work.

"Sure, Rock. If you need the hangar, it's no problem."

"I knew I could count on you," he grinned.

I stepped back before he could slap me again.

"I've got a student now so I'll leave you to it," I said.

He flashed me thumbs up. "Thanks a million, pal."

Later, I told Henry about my conversation with the Citabria buyer.

"So you feel that Rock thinks he is three steps ahead of the government and it's not going to find out about it?"

"Yeah, exactly," I replied.

"Well, when he gets into trouble, let's make sure the problems are his and not ours."

Chapter Six

Saved by the Belle

Henry organized the banner equipment and hung it along the inside of the hangar walls. He announced the results during a coffee break. "The 250 letters we purchased are actually 217 complete letters, numbers and punctuation. There are 23 torn letters and a pile of red scraps."

"Is there a complete alphabet?" I asked.

"We have at least one of each letter but most of the vowels are in the damaged pile," he replied. "Leanne, would you like more coffee?"

"Sure," she said and started to get up.

Her husband popped out of his chair. "Stay there, honey, I'll get it."

Leanne looked surprised but willingly handed him her cup. Henry was considerate of his wife but only when his one-track mind wasn't tracking something else. He poured her coffee, stood there for a moment and then asked, "What do you take in your coffee?"

Leanne smiled, "Just black."

Henry walked the cup over to her. "There you go, my dear."

"Thank you, my dear," she answered musically.

I hadn't noticed before, but I guessed this was a big event.

Leanne saw the look on my face. "He needs a favour," she explained.

"Not always," Henry protested.

Leanne sipped her coffee and smiled at me. "But not always."

Henry pulled a piece of ripped red cloth from his pocket. He leaned over and handed it to Leanne. "Do you think this could be stitched on your sewing machine?"

Our receptionist took the cloth, rubbed it between her fingers and then held it up to the light. "I think so," she replied.

"It's banner material. If it'll work on your machine, we could patch some of the damaged letters."

Leanne's smile widened. "Sure, I'd be happy to teach you how to run it," she said, holding up her cup, "as long as the job comes with regular coffee service."

Henry looked at me for help. I pretended to study the ceiling.

"Did you know that some of these acoustic tiles are different?" I commented to no one in particular.

Henry turned to his wife and cleared his throat. "I thought we could bring your machine in. You could sew on office time," he said hopefully.

"Have you seen me sitting here doing nothing?" she asked. She was still smiling but her tone was less friendly.

"No," Henry answered quickly, "but sometimes you're just cleaning, talking to customers or answering the phone. I thought you could fit in some sewing."

Leanne's smile slid off her face. "Well, you clean the airplanes, chat up the customers and answer the phone too," Leanne replied. "You could squeeze in the sewing and I'll find the time to teach you."

Leanne was leading my partner into a big hole of his own making. I stood up. "I'll go outside and see if the shingles on the roof are all the same," I announced.

"You don't get off that easily," Leanne declared. The ex-school teacher pointed me back into my seat.

I sat down.

Henry searched for the right words. He didn't find them but he spoke anyway. "The time I spend on the airplanes and with customers is important to our business," he said.

That was it. He had jumped into the hole. I slouched to make myself as small as possible but the explosion was averted. Summer McDay bounded into the office as if on cue.

"Hi, everybody!"

The perky co-ed's greeting was enthusiastic, as always.

She looked around and absorbed the negative vibes. The sunny expression on her face faded. "Am I interrupting something?" she asked quickly.

"No, not at all," Leanne replied. She held up the red cloth. "We were just discussing whether this banner material could be repaired on a regular sewing machine."

Summer closed the door, walked over to Leanne's desk and reached for the fabric.

Summer was studying sports medicine at the local university. She was an overachiever who was easily bored. To keep busy, she worked for us part-time on the flight desk and traded her pay for flying lessons.

She rubbed the shiny red material between her thumb and fingers. "This could be stitched on a home machine," she said. "It's light-weight material. Anyone could sew it."

Leanne laughed. "Thank you young lady. You have answered two questions: would it work on a regular machine and who could sew it?"

"I could!" Summer offered quickly. "I'll bring my machine from the dorm and sew this while I'm covering the desk."

Before Leanne could speak, Henry said, "That's a great idea, Summer. And we'd be happy to pay rent on your sewing machine."

"Oh, that's OK. I never use it. Mom bought it for me to save money on clothes but I only wear sweats or hospital greens to school."

"Well, you don't know how much we appreciate your offer," Henry added. "Come on out to the hangar. I'll show you the rest of the equipment."

Henry opened the door for Summer and looked back with a big grin. Leanne held up her right hand and formed a small space between her thumb and index finger. The unspoken message was clear: you were this close to losing your skin.

"I think I'll join them," I said rising out of my chair.

"Suit yourself," Leanne said in a mock tough-guy voice. Her smile was growing back.

Chapter Seven

Buzz job

Don Hitchcock had ordered his new Super Cub from Buzz Billings. Billings was the Piper Aircraft distributor for our area. I had already sampled the man's oily reputation. You could count on Billings to look after himself in every deal. Nobody kissed his butt. He kissed it himself.

Billings phoned The Flying Circus three days before our open house. I took the call.

"Hi... ah... Buzz Billings here. The Super Cub has arrived."

"That's great, Buzz," I replied. "Can we expect delivery by the end of the week?"

The salesman drew a large breath and then spoke quickly. "There's taxes to pay, registration, Bill of Sale, an import inspection, new wing and, of course, we can't release the airplane until it's paid in full."

His hesitation at the beginning made me wary. "The taxes aren't due right away, Buzz, and the paperwork should have been done in advance. You charge for import inspections but never actually do them. The money is ready so there should be no hold-up. What's this about a new wing?"

"Ah... I have to order a new wing," he mumbled. "It'll take a while to get here."

"Buzz, this isn't sounding good. What's wrong with the wings on it?"

"One's bent, a little," he replied.

"What!"

"It arrived damaged," he said quietly.

"How damaged?"

"The boys are taking it off now."

We found out later that Billings had "hired" an inexperienced pilot to ferry the airplane from the factory to his operation in Toronto. The kid

The Cub snapped left in one almighty ground loop.

was building flying time toward a Commercial Pilot Licence. He actually paid Billings $10 per flying hour and covered his own expenses on the trip. He had never flown a Super Cub before.

The youngster made it to the circuit at Toronto's Mayhem Airport without crashing. He tried to land on a runway that had a strong crosswind. The Cub got away from him after he touched down. A gust picked up the left wing. The Cub snapped left in one almighty ground loop. The right wing hit the asphalt as the right landing gear leg folded inward under the fuselage. The airplane stopped on the edge of the runway pointing backward, one wing up and the other down. The kid browned his pants but was not hurt.

Billings blamed the young pilot and absolved himself as if that would make us happy.

"When will it be fixed, Buzz?"

"Well... the factory doesn't have spare wings. They have to make one and won't start until they complete this final production run of Cubs."

"How long?"

"Six weeks."

"Six weeks!"

"Yes, they'll start on the wing in six weeks. When it arrives here, we'll be ready to cover, paint and install it."

I knew Buzz's six weeks would turn into twelve. "The banner towing season will be half over!" I complained.

"Well, as soon as I receive the balance owing on the airplane, I'll order the wing."

"Buzz, the final payment is not due until the airplane is delivered."

"Well... ah... it has been delivered."

I realized that Billings was squeezing us.

"Why don't you get another new Cub off the line?"

"They're all sold," he replied quickly.

"They may be spoken for but I bet there's a dealer who will sell his delivery position."

"If there is, who's going to pay for it?"

"I'm trying to be helpful, Buzz."

"Just tell your customer that the airplane's here. As soon as he pays for it, we'll work on getting it over there as soon as possible."

"He's your customer, Buzz, you tell him." I hung up.

I called Don Hitchcock right away. He was in a meeting. I left a message, "Don't agree to anything Billings says."

I was alone with the Cub problem. Henry had left early that morning on a cross-country flight. Leanne was running errands downtown while I

I was alone with the Cub problem.

was between students.

I dug out our copy of Hitchcock's sales agreement with Billings. The dealer was in the driver's seat. The agreement did not specify a delivery or closing date.

I telephoned Russ Landsdown, the agent who handled the insurance for The Flying Circus. The Super Cub was not on our policy yet, but Russ's insurance brain had helped us before. He took my call right away.

"Hi there. Did the Super Cub arrive to replace the Citabria?" the cheerful agent asked. "I'm always happy to cover a more expensive airplane."

"Not yet, Russ, and it may be later than sooner," I replied. "That's why I called. I need some advice."

"Shoot."

I told him about the damaged wing on the Cub and my conversation with Billings.

"That sounds like Buzz," Russ said. "I can guess what he's doing. If Don Hitchcock doesn't pay for the airplane now, which he shouldn't, Buzz will be forced to spend his own money to pay Piper. There will also be sales tax due. Whether Hitchcock pays or not, the repairs on the Cub won't cost Buzz anything. He'll claim the accident on his insurance. Then he'll bid low on the repair job. He can still make money because he pays wholesale for Piper parts and his mechanics will work on it only when they have spare time."

"Time is our problem. The clock is ticking on the summer banner towing season."

"I'll tell you what to do but you didn't hear it from me."

"Hey, if it makes me look smart, I won't say a word."

"Good. We'll work a squeeze play of our own. Call the agent who handles Buzz's insurance. I'll give you his name and number. Tell him you are a customer for a Super Cub ordered through Billings but it's bent. Ask him if Buzz's insurance will cover the damage. He won't answer you but his next call will be to Buzz to find out what's going on."

I was taking notes and grinning at the same time.

"Then, talk to your maintenance guy, Darcy Philips. Ask him to call the same insurance agent to inquire about bidding on a rebuild job for a Billings' Super Cub wreck. When Buzz hears about competition for the repairs, he might spring into action."

"That's great, Russ, thank you very much."

"You're welcome. Let me know what happens."

He gave me the insurance agent's number. I called the man. Russ was right about his reaction. He listened but wouldn't tell me anything. Then I telephoned Darcy Philips.

Darcy was the chief mechanic at Derry Air, a flying school in the next city. Henry and I had met him when we had worked there before starting The Flying Circus. Darcy's shop maintained our aircraft.

I told him about the Cub and asked if he would bid on the rebuild.

"If Billings gets the job," the feisty mechanic said, "you'll be lucky to see that airplane flying this year."

"I know. That's why I appreciate your help moving things along."

"Happy to oblige. Maybe I'll get the repair contract."

"I hope you do."

The phone rang a few minutes later.

"Good afternoon, The Flying Circus."

"You have no business calling my insurance agent!" Billings bellowed.

"It did seem like a mean trick," I replied calmly. "After all, it's your airplane and your insurance."

Billings was ready to argue. My agreement caught him off guard.
"Well, yeah... what do you think you're doing?" he grumbled.
"Just trying to stir up some action, Buzz. We need that airplane now."
"There'll be no action until your man pays for it."
"It won't happen, Buzz. Not until he can fly it."
"Then he'll lose his deposit."
"No deposit is better than no airplane."
"You'll be hearing from my lawyer."
"Does he fix Cubs...?"
Billings hung up.

The next call was from Don Hitchcock. "I got your message," the jolly politician said. "What's up?"

I told him the Cub story. "Have you talked to Billings yet?" I asked.

"No, but his is the next message on my desk."

"Well, he's saying the Cub is delivered and he wants you to pay the balance and then he'll order a new wing."

"And if I don't?"

"Then he threatens to forfeit your deposit. He uses the money to fix the airplane and then sells it to someone else."

"Can he afford to pay Piper in the meantime?"

"Probably but he doesn't want to," I replied. "That's why he's pressing for you to pay. The sales tax is also due."

"Hmmm... then we have some leverage," Don mused.

"Well, call him but don't agree to anything," I suggested. "Phone me back, let me know what he says and I'll coach you from there."

"You're talking to a junkyard lawyer who is also a politician and a borderline honest cabinet minister," he giggled. "My granddaddy was a horse trader."

"Well then, he's all yours."

"I'll ring you back."

"Thanks."

Don called again 20 minutes later. "I think we've got him," he chuckled. "I gave him two weeks to have a new, flyable Super Cub delivered to your ramp."

"But he can't do that even if he wanted to."

"I know. I told him I'd sue him for my deposit plus lost revenue on the airplane. Then I said I'd talk to my seatmate in the legislature, the Minister of Revenue, about a sales tax audit of his company. That made him squeak."

"Sounds like you cornered him but how does that speed the delivery?"

"I gave him a third alternative," Don replied. I could hear a cheesy grin in his voice. "He can deliver the airplane and the damaged wing to Derry Air by Friday for Darcy Philips to repair. I told him that I'd pay him in full by the end of the month, minus Darcy's bill."

"What did he say?"

"Nothing, but I could hear heavy breathing. I told him to call me by noon tomorrow with a decision and then I hung up."

"Ahh... Don, Darcy can't get a new wing for us any faster than Billings can."

"Can't he fix the damaged one or find a good used wing?"

"I don't know. I'll talk to him."

"OK, thanks. Call me back."

"Hi, Darcy."

"Hey, it's The Flying Circus clown. What have you wrecked now?"

"Nothing but Don Hitchcock thinks you're a miracle worker."

"What can I say? When you're good, you're good."

"It sounds like Don cornered Buzz Billings into delivering the damaged Cub to you for repairs. If you can do it, Don will pay you and deduct the cost from what he owes Billings for the airplane."

"Hey, your guy is smart."

"What about fixing the airplane?"

"No problem. Good Cub wings are scarce, but if we can't find what we need," he laughed, "we'll shorten the left wing and use those parts on the right side. You'll just have to tow smaller banners."

"Very funny."

"When is the Cub being delivered?"

"Maybe Friday. I'll have to let you know."

"Good stuff. Leave the Cub to me. We can fix anything. In the meantime, you learn some advertising abbreviations."

"Smart guy."

"I can't help it."

I called Don Hitchcock back and told him that Darcy had said the repairs would be no problem.

"That's great," he replied.

I could hear the ice cubes rattle in the politician's drink.

"I just got off the phone with Buzz Billings. He'll send the wounded Cub to Derry Air on a trailer on Friday. I had to agree that the repairs would not exceed my deposit on the airplane, otherwise he would be claiming the accident on his insurance, slowing everything down."

"But we won't know the repair cost until Darcy sees the airplane."

"You said he was good," he snorted. "Here's his chance to prove it."

"I hope it works."

"Don't worry about it. Are you picking me up on Friday in the Mayflower?"

Mayflower was Don's nickname for his Citabria.

"Yes, sir, I'll be there."

"I'll see you then."

I rang Darcy again. "OK miracle worker, the Super Cub will be delivered to you on Friday."

"Thanks chum. I'll get on the horn and scare up some parts."

"There's one catch. Hitchcock agreed that the repairs would not exceed the cost of his deposit."

"No problem. If it's under, we jack up our rates. If it's over, I'll bill Billings for the difference."

"He won't pay it," I replied.

"We are his best Piper parts customer. We'll take it in trade."

"This whole thing is getting too complicated," I complained.

"Now you're sounding like a pilot," the mechanic laughed. "Just leave the repairs to me. You go break something else. I like the business."

"Thanks, I think."

"You're welcome."

The telephone wars had worn me out. I sat there listening to the ringing in my head. Two minutes later, Leanne walked into the office.

"Thanks for holding the fort," she said cheerfully. "Anything happen while I was gone?"

"Not a thing," I sighed.

"I can see that. You look like you're falling asleep. Well, now you can get back to work. Here comes your next student."

Chapter Eight

Cub napping

Darcy Philips stole the Super Cub. The pint-sized mechanic told us about the caper at the open house the next day.

"There was no sign of the Cub being delivered by Friday afternoon. I phoned Buzz a couple of times but he wouldn't take my calls. The receptionist said that the Cub was still in the hangar on a trailer. Buzz gets stubborn like that when he doesn't get his way."

Darcy said that after work on Friday, he drove his vintage Fargo pick-up truck home, loaded his wife and three young kids into the cab and drove to Toronto.

"They love seeing the big city lights," Darcy said with a laugh. "It's cheap entertainment and my wife can't say I don't take her anywhere."

According to Darcy, the Billings hangar was locked up when he arrived. "There was no one around so I hooked a flex-pipe to the truck's exhaust and stuck the other end under the hangar door. Then I revved up the old Fargo with the hand throttle. We had a family picnic in the truck while waiting. The kids ate sandwiches and watched the airplanes landing and taking off while my wife and I listened to tunes."

Darcy said he removed the pipe when the exhaust smoke began seeping out around the hangar doors. "I drove the truck over to the edge of the ramp and called in the alarm from a payphone." His grin turned devilish as he spoke.

"The airport fire trucks roared up to the hangar. Those guys had the door open in no time. Boy, I wish I had some of their equipment!"

Darcy followed the firemen into the hangar. "The smoke was thinnest at floor level so I ducked down. I could see the Cub parked along one wall. The wings were off and everything was secured on a trailer. I couldn't believe my luck."

The cheeky mechanic started to push a couple of the aircraft from in front of the Cub outside. "The firemen were running around looking for the source of the smoke but one of them helped me move airplanes out. I backed the truck, family included, into the smoky hangar. The guy hitched the Cub trailer to my truck," the gutsy mechanic chuckled. "He gave me a thumbs up. I waved and drove away."

"I waved and drove away."

Chapter Nine

Open House

The giant red banner faced the highway from the back of our hangar. Henry and I had made it by clipping aerial advertising letters together. It was seven feet high and 100 feet long.

FLYING CIRCUS OPEN HOUSE SAT 10-3

I drove to work early on the day of the open house. The sunrise painted a glow on everything facing east, including the red sign. Seeing it made me feel good about our flying business. Things were looking up; the open house would generate new customers and we would be earning extra revenue from banner towing.

There were two cars and a pick-up truck already in the parking lot. The cars belonged to Henry and Leanne. Chainsaw Charlie's mother owned the truck. Charlie was the 14-year-old Grade 8 student who helped out around The Flying Circus. He was allowed to drive the truck to the airport in exchange for helping at home with his seven younger brothers and sisters. The police never stopped Charlie for driving under age. He was a dark-haired, six-foot tall, muscular 200-pounder who could pass for the father of three. His nickname came from his lumberjack clothes and the fact that he had built an airplane with plywood and a chainsaw.

"She sure went together quick," Charlie told us, "but by the time I mounted the tractor diesel in her, she was too heavy to fly."

Chainsaw, Henry and Leanne were already washing and vacuuming our four airplanes.

"Looking good!" I called out, "but you're not done. I should have come later!"

"Grab a bucket," Leanne replied, "I've never seen you clean before!"

We were ready by ten o'clock. Al Milton had arrived wearing a chef's hat and an apron that read, "Mr. Excitement". Summer McDay and

Chainsaw Charlie had dusted three lime lines across the active runway to mark the landing spot. They were loading lawn chairs in Chainsaw's truck to take out beside the runway where they would score the contest. The first entrants were taxiing out in our two Cherokees.

Summer's brother, Barry McDay, was cleaning the windows on our Cessna 172. Barry was an air traffic controller in the Circus Tower. He was also a commercial pilot who flew for The Flying Circus part-time. Barry would be flying sightseers and giving introductory lessons in the high-wing Cessna during the open house before beginning his shift in the control tower at three o'clock.

Al Milton called me over. He waved a spatula at the grill and the food table. "Am I expected to do all this by myself?"

I didn't answer right away. Al was constantly joking. I had learned to hold back until I could tell where the conversation was going. "Why do you ask, Al?"

"Well, I should have an assistant," he declared. "That ape-man Charlie fella doesn't need that chick's help. I'm an old man," he chuckled. "She should be working under me."

"You're an old man all right, a dirty old man. Forget about Summer. She's young enough to be your daughter."

"Oh yeah, what was her mother's maiden name?"

The weather was good. A moderate wind was blowing from the southwest but a bright sun was winning its fight against the early spring chill. Henry and I set up two aircraft display areas. We parked the Citabria on the ramp for showing to the general public. Near it, we roped off a section of grass and posted a sign that read, "Reserved for A-FOOL".

Darcy Philips drove onto the ramp in his pick-up truck pulling a trailer. He stopped and stuck his head out the window. "Somebody said there's a barbeque here. I've got three hungry monsters and an airplane that followed us from Toronto."

Henry and I walked over to greet him.

"We weren't expecting you or the Cub today," I replied in surprise.

"Darn, do I need an invitation?"

"No, you don't," Henry answered from the other side of the truck. "You're welcome here any time." He opened the passenger door and helped the three youngsters, all under six, down from their seat.

We walked behind the truck to see the Cub. It was hard to miss. The whole airplane was a shiny, bright yellow. Apparently the last few aircraft off the assembly line were painted the same as the first ones 50 years earlier. The Cub's wings were strapped along each side of the fuselage. The damaged right side landing gear was resting on a milk crate. One of the wing tips was bent up. Its fabric covering was split and peeled back.

Henry looked at it closely. "Is it repairable?" he asked Darcy.

"Probably," the mechanic chuckled. "The visibility was bad when I first saw it last night and I was kinda in a hurry."

Then he told us the rest of the story.

"Well, we have a spot for it," Henry said motioning to the roped off area of grass.

"Maybe we could stick a sign on the damaged side," Darcy joked, "'Wrecked Super Cub courtesy of Billings Aviation.'"

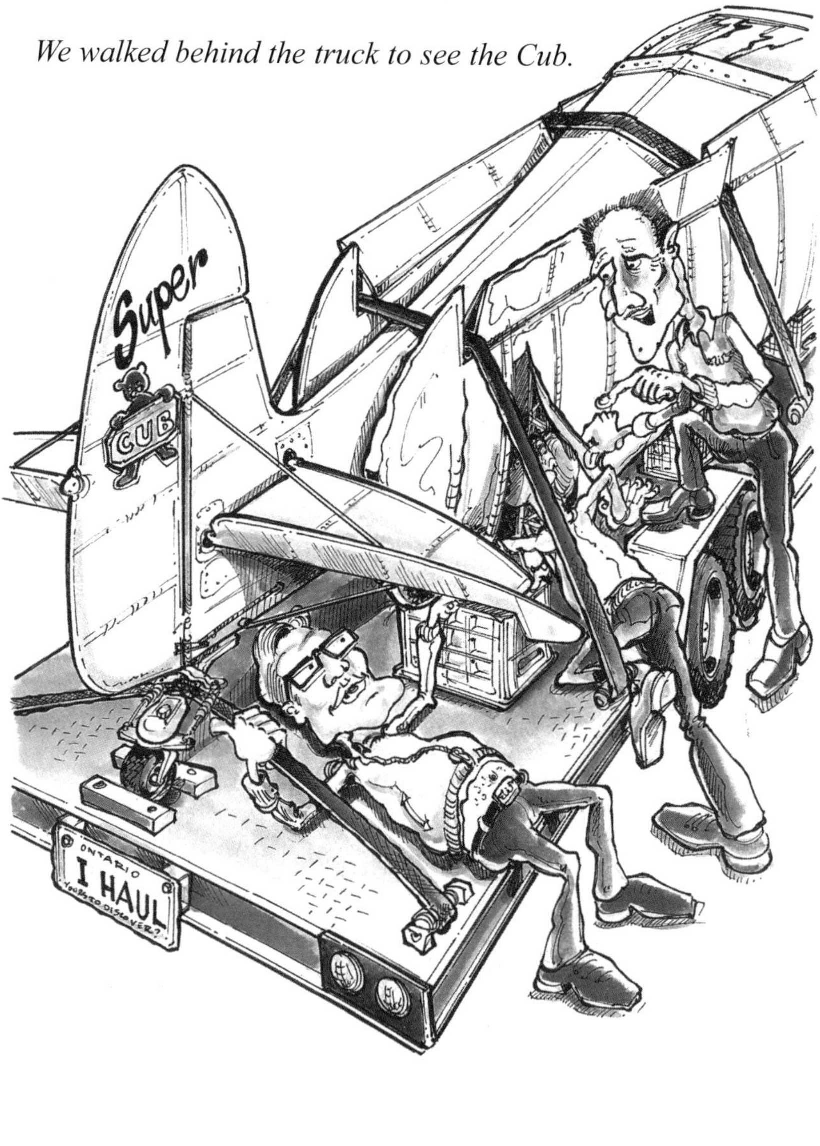

We walked behind the truck to see the Cub.

Chapter Ten

April Fool

Rock Headley arrived at the open house in a grey mini-van. The car didn't fit his California image. Neither did his passengers. Rock's wife, two young kids and his mother piled out of the van and followed him to the ramp. Henry and I greeted them.

I had met Rock's mother when she had paid for his flying lessons. Rock introduced her and the rest of his family.

"You've met my mother, Bella," he said. The older woman nodded in our direction. "This is the wife, Sandy." Rock reached back and patted the pretty, petite blond on the head. "And this is Roxanne and Rock Junior." He pointed to the two little kids clinging shyly to their mother's tight white pants.

Rock looked around the ramp. "We came to see the new Challenger business jet," he grinned.

Henry immediately excused himself. "I'll let my partner take care of you," he said quickly. "Nice to meet you all. Enjoy the open house." He walked toward the hangar.

Rock frowned. "I don't see a Challenger."

"No, but the new Super Cub is here," I said, as if it was nearly the same. "Come on, I'll show you."

Rock stood firm. "A Super Cub is not a business jet," he declared. "I promised the kids that they'd see a jet."

"Well..." I stammered, "it... it hasn't arrived yet." And never will, I said to myself.

Rock's frown deepened. "When will it get here?"

"We don't know but how about showing the family the Citabria that you purchased?" I suggested hopefully.

"I will," he snapped, "but I want to see the Challenger. Where is it?"

My brain was scrambling for a good way to handle this.

"There was a hold-up painting the aircraft registration letters," I offered, "A-F-O-O-L?"

Rock leaned his face closer to mine. "Are you telling me that I dragged the family out here to see a jet and it isn't coming?"

He sounded gruff, the veins in his thick neck were swelling and his biceps bulged under his T-shirt. Rock's wife touched the back of his sleeve as if to indicate he should tone it down. The kids squirmed at her side. Rock ignored them.

I decided he would either blow up or wise up; there would be no in between.

"For April Fools Day, Rock, I might tell you crazy things that you shouldn't believe."

A smile spread across his large tanned face. He slapped my shoulder. I staggered sideways.

"April Fool to you too," Rock laughed. "I had you going good there, didn't I?"

Rock's mother smiled. His wife shook her head back and forth. He had either been pulling my leg or he had just caught on. I'll never know.

"Yes, Rock," I replied, rubbing my shoulder, "you did have me going."

"Now, let's see the Super Cub," he said.

We walked to the trailer. Rock looked at the wing damage. "Looks like you need a new right wing."

Darcy came over with his three kids before I could answer. I made the introductions.

"So you're the fella who's going to fix this thing?" Rock asked.

"That's me," Darcy replied. "As long as these guys are flying, I'll be fixing."

"I've got some Super Cub parts including a right wing that you might use," Rock said casually.

Darcy gave me a questioning look. I shrugged as if I didn't know anything about it. I didn't. Rock was full of surprises.

"I've been collecting airplane parts to start a fly-in fishing camp," Rock explained. "I have a wing from a damaged Cub."

"I might like to see it," Darcy replied in a cautious tone. "What year was the Cub?"

"I don't know," Rock said. He smiled and pointed to the bent wing. "It looks like this one only straighter. Let me know if you're interested and maybe we can make a deal."

"Give me a minute," Darcy replied. He hopped onto the trailer, opened a knife that he produced from nowhere and slit the fabric further from the tear. He looked inside and then pulled his head out. "I'm interested."

Darcy slit the fabric further and looked inside.

"We can go to my house and you can check it out," Rock offered.

Darcy jumped off the trailer. "Do you have a price in mind?"

Rock answered in a cool, macho voice. "Ah, you can have it," he said, "I'm happy to help."

I couldn't believe my ears.

Darcy let the offer float for a moment and then said, "I can have it in exchange for what?"

Rock turned toward the Citabria parked on the ramp. "Well, I bought that Citabria and I'm going to put her on floats." He looked at Darcy to see his reaction. "I might need some help from an engineer signing some stuff off."

"I bet you will," Darcy grinned. "Let's go and we'll talk on the way."

The five kids were playing together in the grass. Rock pulled out a fat roll of twenty-dollar bills and peeled one off the top. "You and mom buy the kids some lunch here," he said to his wife, "I won't be long."

Sandy took the money but kept her hand out. "Do your mom and I get lunch?"

Rock frowned and gave her another twenty.

Sandy turned to Darcy. "The kids are having fun together. I'll watch all of them while you go with Rock."

"That would be great," he replied.

She extended her hand toward Darcy and said, "I'd be happy to buy them lunch, too."

It was the first time I had seen the cock-sure mechanic blush. He fumbled for his wallet and gave her $20. "Thanks very much," he replied.

I was seeing a Sandy who was not a timid mouse.

She smiled at Darcy. "You're welcome."

Rock turned and started walking toward the parking lot.

Darcy bent down and told his kids what was happening and that he would be back soon.

He stood up. I touched his arm and quietly said, "Darcy, you don't want to get involved with this guy. His floats are oversize and they don't match."

The mechanic smiled. "I understand, and the Cub wing and his floats might be hot, maybe not. That's why I want to 'help' him."

"I don't get it."

"I'm not surprised," he grinned. "I like to work with guys like Rock. It keeps me in touch with the aviation underground and maybe we'll get your Cub flying sooner."

I shook my head. "I hope you know what you're doing."

"No worries. Me and Rock come from the same kind of place."

"You do?"

"Yeah," he replied. "The school of hard knocks." Then he smacked me on my shoulder as if he was Rock and trotted off, smiling.

Chapter Eleven

Naked dancing

I had instructed Chainsaw Charlie to lay a wide trail of lime and two thin ones across Runway 24. The fat line was just beyond the 500-foot marks. One skinny line ran across 100 feet short of that and the other, 100 feet beyond.

I briefed Chainsaw and Summer on how to score the landing contest. "The aim is for the pilots to land their main wheels on the big line. Bounces and nosewheel landings score zero. So does landing outside the 200-foot box created by the two thin lines. Then you just measure the distance from the main line of each landing inside the box." I handed them each a sheet of contest rules. "It's all on here."

"What if they all miss the box?" the big youngster asked.

I smiled. "That would never happen at a flying school as good as The Flying Circus."

"Whatever you say, boss."

"Good. And will you please bring in the score sheet every hour so the pilots can see how they're doing."

"OK."

Two pilots renting our Cherokees were the only entrants during the first half hour of the contest. They must have enjoyed themselves. They each booked another slot for later that morning when they returned. Then two customers with their own aircraft joined in. Soon some flying club members dropped by our office to pay their ten dollars for three landings. A few bought multiple entries. A couple of transient pilots taxied over to our ramp and asked if they could enter. Leanne signed them up.

I was happy to see the contest catching on. Even the air traffic controllers on duty were into it. I could see that both guys in the tower had binoculars trained toward the beginning of the runway.

Chainsaw bounced his pick-up truck across the airport infield to deliver the first hour's results. He parked and walked over to me. "Nobody landed inside the box," he said handing me the score sheet.

"I'm surprised."

"The landings are all over the runway but never near the line," he added, "and lots of bounces."

"Well, I haven't heard any complaints so we won't worry about it yet."

I looked at the sheet. The score column was all zeros. I posted it on the outside of the office.

"Who's winning?" Henry asked.

"They're all tied for last."

The office radio monitor was set up next to the barbeque. The unmistakably loud voice of Melville Passmore boomed across the ramp.

"Circus Tower, TriPacer Charlie Lima Oscar Whiskey November, approaching the control zone from the west, landing at Circus."

This was followed by three seconds of sidetone and then Melville clicked off.

"TriPacer Lima Oscar Whiskey November," the controller replied, "you are cleared for a right downwind for Runway 24, wind 230 at 15, altimeter 30.01. Watch for four aircraft in the left-hand circuit."

"Lima Oscar Whiskey November, roger."

Melville landed, taxied in and parked his colourful airplane off to one side of our ramp. The right hand door popped open. Melville hopped out and ran toward me just like he had two weeks ago.

"This is the big day!" he shouted. Several customers turned to see who was yelling. "I'm getting married!" he whooped.

The farm boy almost bowled me over. His was really excited. He stopped in front of me, grabbed my hand and gave it a vigorous shake.

"You're my best, best man," he declared loudly.

"Am I not your only best man?"

"That's what I said! Did you remember a monkey suit?"

I laughed. "Yes sir, it's in my car."

"I'm excited!" He was literally dancing on the end of our handshake.

"Did you hit the spot when you landed here?" I asked.

That took some wind out of his sails. He stopped dancing and let go of my hand. His face turned pink.

"What's the matter?"

Melville looked down at his feet. "I was gonna," he mumbled.

"Why didn't you?"

"Well, I set up for a short field glide approach but..."

"Yes?"

"She's not dancing, she's doing aerobics."

"There was a girl dancing beside the runway." The pink in his face darkened. His voice dropped. "She didn't have any clothes on."

"What?"

I knew Summer McDay was out by the runway but I couldn't imagine her dancing naked. Actually, I could imagine it but I didn't believe it.

"I'll have to check into this, Melville. Help yourself to food and drinks."

"OK, good idea!" He sounded relieved to drop the subject.

Before I could organize getting out to the beginning of Runway 24, Chainsaw arrived with the second hour's results. I hustled over to the truck.

"Still zeros," he said. "Even Barry tried and missed the box at the end of a sightseeing flight."

"I think I know why. Tell me, what is Summer doing out there?"

"Nothing. There's nothing to do until someone lands in the box."

"Is she dressed?"

His head rocked back in surprise. "Ah, yeah!"

"Is she dancing?"

The youngster gave me a strange look and then said. "No, she's not dancing." Then he began to smile. "Well, she's doing aerobics."

"But she's not naked?"

"No!" he exclaimed, then he added, "she just took her sweats off."

"So she is naked!"

"No! She's wearing a sports bra and Spandex shorts."

I could picture the sports medicine student gyrating to keep active.

"She's in good shape," Chainsaw grinned sheepishly.

"One of the pilots said she didn't have any clothes on," I said.

Charlie tossed his head back and laughed. "That's a good one. Her shorts and top are tan coloured."

The image was complete. I laughed too.

"Well, tell little Miss Jumping Jack from me that the sweats go back on. She's wrecking our contest."

"OK boss," he smiled. "Can I grab some drinks and grub first?"

"Absolutely. And take a bag of ice cubes and dump them on your over-heated helper."

Chapter Twelve

Spot on

Rock and Darcy returned in the van. They walked toward the Cub on the trailer talking and laughing like old friends. I was with a customer so it was a few minutes before I went over to join them. By then, Rock had left with his family and Henry was talking to Darcy.

"The muscleman's wing will do," Darcy was saying as I approached, "so I made a deal with him."

"What kind of deal?" Henry frowned.

"We're trading wings and I'm signing off his modifications on the Citabria."

Henry winced.

I spoke. "Isn't the newer wing worth more?"

"Not with the spar bent."

"I hope you didn't make promises you don't want to keep," Henry advised.

"Hey, no worries," Darcy grinned, "it's the opposite. Before today, Rocko was modifying stuff in his backyard on his own. Now I'll be supervising. It should make his version of airworthiness closer to mine."

A few minutes later a mustard-faced Melville found me. He swiped a sleeve across his mouth and said, "I'll fly the spot landing contest now. Then I'll be ready to go when you are."

"OK. Good luck."

"I don't need it. I'm goin' to win!"

"Well, this is supposed to be your big day."

The happy farmer ambled off to his airplane.

I walked to the barbeque and asked Al Milton for a steak-on-a-bun.

"Coming right up," the jolly jokester replied. "That's two dollars for the steak, two for the bun and two more if you want a plate. That comes to eight dollars."

I gave him a $10 bill. "With your math, you must be making money hand over fist!"

"All for a good cause, my man." He stuffed the bill in his apron. "Thanks for the tip."

Melville's voice boomed out of the radio monitor. He was asking for taxi instructions for the spot landing contest. The controller cleared him to Runway 24.

Later, I heard the young pilot call on the downwind leg for a stop and go landing on the spot. I looked up. The brightly coloured TriPacer was turning onto a base leg. I finished eating my steak-on-a-bun and watched Melville approach the runway. His set-up looked good. He was high but the TriPacer was sinking rapidly in its trademark elevator approach. The wind had picked up so the airplane appeared to be descending almost straight down.

The nose started up as Melville crossed the threshold of the runway. I was too far away to see the temporary lines but if Chainsaw's pick-up was parked beside the target then Melville was going to land close to it.

The TriPacer flared but the main wheels hit hard. I saw brief puffs of smoke come from the tires. The airplane continued down the runway with a shower of sparks trailing from the landing gear. It stopped in less distance than I thought possible.

The air traffic controller's voice on the frequency monitor broke my concentration. "Lima Oscar Whiskey November, do you require assistance?"

There was a long pause before Melville answered. "Ah... I... I don't know. I hafta call back."

The tower controller instructed the next two airplanes in the circuit to stay at 1,000 feet because of an aircraft on the runway.

From where I was standing, it looked like the TriPacer's propeller had stopped. I could see Chainsaw Charlie trotting toward the airplane and then Melville climbing out. They both looked at the wheels.

A few minutes later, Melville's voice stammered over the radio. "I... I guess I need some h... help."

By now everyone on the ramp was listening. Darcy split the air with a two-fingered whistle. I looked his way. He waved me toward his truck. I hustled over. Henry joined us. The mechanic motioned for us to get in. He started the engine.

"Come on," he barked, "we'll drive out there."

Henry and I hopped into the front seat. Darcy let out the clutch on the old Fargo and headed for the taxiway.

"The guy in the tower is keeping the traffic in the air," Darcy offered.

Chainsaw leaned on the strut while Melville performed an agitated dance.

It was his explanation for not taking the slow bumpy route across the infield. He turned onto the active taxiway and blasted toward Runway 24.

It was obvious that Darcy's classic truck did not have a stock drive-train. He powered around the corner onto the runway and roared toward the TriPacer.

"What's he doing so close to the edge of the runway?" Darcy asked. "Who taught this guy how to fly?"

I knew that he knew the answer to his second question.

"It's a long story," I replied.

Chainsaw was leaning on the right wing strut while Melville was performing an agitated dance in front of him. There were bare rims where the main tires should have been. Twin grooves in the asphalt led from the rims back to the spot landing line at the edge of the runway.

Darcy wheeled the truck around and backed it in front of the airplane. The three of us jumped out. The mechanic was the first one to Melville. He put his arm around the chubby farmer's shoulders. I stood back. Henry walked over to look at the landing gear.

"Looks like those tires gave out on the landing," Darcy said for all to hear. "I guess we should have changed them at the inspection last month." He steered Melville toward the back of the pick-up truck. "Come on, give me a hand."

Darcy dropped the Fargo's tailgate and dragged out a triangular hangar dolly from the mound of stuff he always carried. He dropped it onto the tarmac. "Here, roll this over to the left main gear," he said to Melville. "We'll get these three goons to lift on the struts so you can slide it under."

We got the message and walked around to the left side. Darcy hauled out another dolly, let it drop on the ground, shoved it toward the right wheel and then joined us.

"Chainsaw, I want you to squat down and stick your head between the struts like this so you've got one strut on each shoulder." Darcy demonstrated what he wanted the youngster to do. Then he stepped aside. "And Melville, when we lift up, you roll the dolly under the axle."

With that, Chainsaw slowly stood up between the struts, lifting the wing before we could help.

"Go ahead, Melville," Darcy said without missing a beat.

The farm boy knelt down with his tongue hanging out in concentration and positioned the centre of the dolly under the damaged rim.

"OK, let her down Chainsaw. Perfect. Now the other side."

Within a few minutes Darcy had the front of the TriPacer roped to the trailer hitch on the truck. He instructed Melville to sit in his airplane for the ride to the ramp. Chainsaw walked back to join Summer at the spot landing line. Henry and I climbed into the truck cab with Darcy. He let out the clutch and inched slowly along the runway to the taxiway.

"That was pretty slick," I said to Darcy. "You kept Melville busy while hustling the airplane off the runway. When did you become a psychologist?"

Darcy grinned and checked his rearview mirror. "I get child psychology lessons every day at home and at work. I have three kids, six mechanics and 12 pilots to look after not counting you guys. The learning does not take long."

"I'm impressed."

"When we get to the ramp," Darcy said, "it's your turn to keep Melville busy and to get him to the church in time for his wedding."

"How do you know about the wedding?"

"You're not the only one invited," he replied, mimicking an uppercrust voice. "He has other friends in aviation."

"I was going to fly home with him in the TriPacer," I thought aloud.

"Take the Citabria," Henry offered. "I'll fuel it for you."

"Thanks."

It was three o'clock.

Keeping Melville busy worked. Darcy told the young farmer that he'd take care of the TriPacer. "I'll see you at the wedding," he told him. "Make sure you're there on time or I'll take your place next to that pretty bride of yours."

I snatched my suit bag from the Volkswagen and hustled the worried pilot over to the Citabria. He helped me push it to the edge of the taxiway and complete a pre-flight inspection.

"You fly from the front seat," I said.

"I... I've never flown one of these things," he replied nervously.

"It's just another airplane," I assured him. I helped him into the seat and showed him how to fasten the aerobatic seat belts.

"Here's the checklist." I handed him the card. "Follow it and take your time finding everything. I'll be right here behind you."

Melville settled down as he began talking himself through the pre-start checks. He started the engine with occasional prompts from me and called the ground controller for taxi instructions.

"Circus Ground, this is Charlie Lima Oscar Whiskey November at The Flying Circus ready to taxi for a flight."

The controller was Barry McDay. He knew the voice and the airplane. "Hi Melville, this is Circus Ground. I check you're in Citabria Lima Oscar Oscar Papa. You're cleared to taxi to Runway 24, wind 230 at 15, occasionally 20, altimeter 29.98. Taxi via Delta Bravo, hold short of 24."

"Lima Oscar Whiskey November."

"Where are you headed?" Barry asked.

Melville snapped his head around toward me. "What did he say?"

"He wants to know your destination," I replied.

Melville took a deep breath, licked his lips, pulled in his tongue, pushed the microphone button and blurted out what was in his head, "I'm going to get married," he announced nervously.

"I check you're headed for the home strip," Barry replied.

"Affirmative," Melville said into the mic. Then he turned to see my reaction. I nodded in agreement.

Melville stretched to see over the nose-high airplane. He added power and pushed the left rudder to turn up the taxiway. The airplane rolled straight.

"Full rudder, Melville, the tailwheel steering is not as direct as in the TriPacer. Hold the stick all the way back."

The Citabria curved to the left.

"Now full right rudder to stop the turn," I said.

"Whoaaaa!" Melville exclaimed.

We just missed the edge of the asphalt. The Citabria jerked and snaked its way to the runway. Melville stomped on one rudder pedal and then the other while I tap danced on my brake pedals and barked instructions.

Melville completed the rest of the checks out loud and then called for a take-off clearance.

"You're cleared for takeoff, Melville," Barry replied. "Wind 230 at 17. Call clear of the control zone."

"Lima Oscar Whiskey November."

"I'll talk you through the takeoff," I said.

"No, you do it!" he replied quickly.

"You can see forward better than I can from back here but I'll follow you on my controls."

It was true. I could see out both sides and had no trouble flying the Citabria from the back seat but I wanted Melville to feel like he was back in the saddle and in control.

"Line up on the runway, Melville, apply full power, move the control stick forward to lift the tail and be ready with the right rudder pedal. Now go!"

We went.

Melville's experience with farm machinery took over. He guided the Citabria into the air with decreasing oscillations and headed home.

"My stomach feels funny when I think about crashing the TriPacer," he moaned in level flight.

"Well, try thinking about something else. Think that you didn't crash. You just landed hard. Darcy will have that airplane flying soon."

"My stomach is still funny."

"The cows will move when I fly a low pass," Melville said.

"OK, think about the wedding. You're getting married in an hour. We still have to land, change our clothes and get to the church. Now your stomach should be fluttering. Mine is."

"You're right," he said, "but what will Mary Ellen think when I tell her I damaged the airplane?"

"Forget the airplane, Melville. The next time you see Mary Ellen, just say, 'I do!'"

He stopped talking. That was never a good sign with Melville. He confused himself when he thought too much.

"Melville?"

"Yes."

"You're going to land this airplane at your strip."

"I don't know how."

"You will when we're done."

I reflected on the TriPacer accident. I believed I knew what mistake Melville had made but I wanted to be sure before I mentioned it. I leaned forward and told the young pilot how we were going to fly the short field landing in the tailwheel airplane.

"There are no flaps so just slow to 75 mph. Cut the power when you're close enough to glide over the trees. Touchdown in a full stall. Don't let it land until the stick is all the way back. OK?"

"I guess so."

Melville found the strip and flew overhead. It was covered with cows.

"They'll move when I do a low pass," Melville said.

"OK cowboy, you're driving."

The windsock on their shanty hangar was showing a snappy wind favouring the southwest.

"I'll do a low pass with the wind," Melville announced.

I agreed. It would save us time.

He descended, flew a teardrop-shaped approach and a low and over. It was obvious that he was gaining confidence with the Citabria.

I looked down when Melville applied full power on the go-around. The cows were meandering their way to the one side of the strip leaving just enough room for an airplane on the other.

Melville flew another teardrop and lined up facing the runway into the wind. He kept the airplane high on the approach and slowed it to 75 mph.

"This airplane glides further than the TriPacer," I called forward to Melville, "so cut the power now."

I was truthful about the glide but the timing of the power cut was bad advice given on purpose. Melville eased the throttle back and lowered the nose to maintain 75.

We seemed to hang in mid-air as the Citabria descended into the wind. If I had called it right, we'd be a tad short of the trees and the runway.

"It's looking good there, Melville," I lied.

The approach worked out just as I had hoped. The wind reduced our gliding distance. Melville should have added some power to stretch the glide or started an overshoot. He eased the nose up slightly instead without noticing that he was trading airspeed for extra gliding distance. It was a common mistake in windy weather. We skimmed nicely over the trees but the airspeed was down to 70 mph. At that speed, the TriPacer would have dropped like a rock.

"Look at the airspeed!" I barked.

Melville jerked in his seat with surprise. Then he tried to hit full power. That was the correct response in his airplane but I held my duplicate power lever so he couldn't.

"I have control!" I yelled. I eased my control stick all the way back.

The wingspan on the Citabria was five feet wider and the stall speed was five mph slower than the TriPacer. There was enough extra lift to flare out at the lower speed. The airplane politely plopped onto the turf on the three wheels at once.

"Any cows ahead," I asked loudly.

Melville hoisted himself up in his seat to look. "All clear," he shouted. He almost sounded cheerful.

I parked in front of the hangar. "You have control, Melville. All the switches for shutdown are in the front."

"I have control," he sang out.

I waited until he completed the final checks. "You climb out first."

He opened the door and hopped down. He was smiling.

I followed him out. "I hope you're grinning because of the wedding," I said, "because that's next."

"That too," he answered. "You just showed me how I goofed the spot landing, didn't you?"

"I did, if you saw what I saw."

"I remember you told me to lower the nose to go down; raise the nose and go all the way down?"

It was a phrase repeated by instructors teaching glide approaches.

"Hey, you catch on better than the measles," I replied. It was a country phrase borrowed from another pilot.

"Thanks," he said. He grabbed my hand and shook it.

"You're welcome. Now it's four o'clock. Let's get you to the church on time."

Chapter Thirteen

"I do!"

Melville and I made it to the wedding with whole minutes to spare. The church was small and full. About 60 pairs of eyes watched us enter with the minister and take our places standing at the front.

If the groom was nervous, he wasn't showing it. Melville gave a little wave and a big smile to each face he recognized, which was most of them. They individually smiled and waved back.

I couldn't see anyone wearing overalls but the whole congregation looked like farmers in church. Their suits and dresses were neat, tidy and old fashioned. The men's bare heads were tanned and white divided by a cap line above their eyebrows. Most of the ladies' hair-dos were the same. There must have been a special on short, curly perms at the local hairdresser.

I was struck by how comfortable I felt standing in front of these strangers. They didn't appear formal or stuffy, just smiley and down-home nice.

I looked at Melville. There was no mistake; he was a farmer. His new suit didn't fit his bowling ball shape and he had somehow rumpled it between the house and the church.

Then I looked down at myself. I fitted the group better than I had realized. My suit was wrinkled from being thrown into the back of my Volkswagen and then the airplane. It looked like I had tossed it onto my body in our rush to the church, which I had. My shoes were dusty from the landing strip and I caught a lingering whiff of cow odor from being in Melville's car.

The bridal party appeared at the entrance to the church. The minister asked all to rise. The organist hit three high notes and then shifted into the wedding march. The congregation stood and turned to look back.

Melville and I had the best view. The maid of honour was first to enter the aisle. She was a gangly teenager who walked like it was her first time in high heels.

Melville leaned toward me. "That's Mary Ellen's sister," he whispered loudly, "Portia."

Then came the beaming bride on her dad's arm. Her gown was layered sheer material and lace. She walked with confidence and grace. She was beautiful.

"That was her grandmother's wedding dress," Melville whispered again.

I smiled.

"And then it was her mother's."

I moved a clasped hand sideways in a "be quiet" sign but he wasn't looking at me. He was all eyes for Mary Ellen.

The ceremony was country simple. Melville belted out his vows for the whole world to hear. Mary Ellen's voice was quieter but clear and determined. There was a round of applause when the minister presented the newly-weds to the congregation. The maid of honour and I followed them down the aisle. The young girl grabbed my right arm with both hands to steady herself.

"Oops, sorry," she said in a nervous voice.

"You're doing fine," I replied.

We formed a receiving line at the church entrance with the two sets of parents. I shook hands with everyone as they shuffled past. I didn't know a soul but they seemed to know me.

"You must be that flying fella," an older gent said with a whistle and click of his dentures. "Glad to meet ya."

"Thank you."

A short, round lady giggled and gushed, "Melville talks about you all the time."

"Good things, I hope," I replied.

"Oh, Lordy, yes!" she snorted. Then she slapped her hand over her mouth as if she had misspoken in church.

"Is yer plane parked outside?" a young farmer chuckled.

His wife leaned in front of him, "Shush Jeremiah." She grabbed my hand and gave it a pump. "It's a pleasure that you're here," she grinned. "Me and Jeremy always wave at airplanes going over in case it's you and Melville."

"I'll be sure to wave back," I replied.

It didn't take long for the church to empty. It was milking time for most of the folks. The wedding party scattered to their cars for the same reason. I rode back to the Passmore place with Melville. At the house, I was finally introduced to his parents. They were both older versions of their son: short, round, a bit loud but happy. Melville and I changed out of our suits and went to the barn with his dad. They had a parlour set-up for milking. I would have helped but everyone, including the cows, knew the routine. I stood and watched.

Melville hummed happily as he monitored the feed to each cow. His dad stood in the milking pit alternately plugging and unplugging the milking machine to the udders.

"OK, that does it," Melville said about an hour later. "We want to be first at the reception."

We washed up. Melville had already told me that the reception would be at the community centre not far away. "We'll be going in our milking clothes," he had added.

The reception hall was typical of a rural community centre. It was the size of a small hockey arena. Inside, tables and chairs had been set up lengthwise on half of the floor space. I counted five rows of tables with about 20 chairs on each side. It occurred to me that the wedding guests from the church wouldn't fill two tables but I didn't dwell on it. A curved head table faced the rows from the near end. Beyond, the bare half of the hall floor ended at a stage where a disc jockey wearing headphones was already bobbing his head to music.

The smell of home cooking drifted out of the tiny kitchen on the left side. My mouth started to water and my stomach grumbled. Ladies in dresses and smocks were carrying large platters and bowls of food to a row of buffet tables set up along the far side of the hall. I was suddenly hungry.

Mary Ellen arrived behind us with her sister and her parents. They looked totally different dressed in casual clothes. Melville introduced us. They shook my hand like farmers. Portia looked more like a kid in her barn clothes. She smiled nervously at me, revealing a full set of metal-work on her teeth.

We lined up to greet the arriving guests. I spent the next hour introducing myself to the same people from the church plus 100 more. All were dressed casually and many smelled like they had come straight from a barn, which they had.

"So you're that guy who flies with Melville," one farmer said.

"Yes, sir."

"I'm Uncle Wilbur and this is the wife, Eunice."

I had no idea whose uncle he was and I didn't ask. I was too hungry to prolong the conversation.

"Please to meet you both," I replied.

I had forgotten about Darcy Philips coming to the wedding. The mechanic and his wife arrived at the receiving line carrying a shopping bag. I assumed it contained a gift for the bride and groom. Darcy eyed me up and down as he shook my hand. "You're looking like a regular farm boy," he sniffed. "This is my wife, Mimi," he added nodding toward the woman at his side. Mimi looked like a good fit for the cocky mechanic. She was his height and just as lean. Her blond hair was cut short. She looked pretty in her fitted western shirt and pants. Her cowboy stance matched Darcy's.

"Pleased to meet you, Mimi," I said.

"I've heard a lot about you," she replied, shaking my hand firmly.

"From him? It's all a lie."

"You wish!" Darcy laughed.

The wedding party was the last to line up for the buffet but the tables were still groaning with food. I overloaded a plate and carried it to the head table. Uncle Wilbur stood up as I sat down. He was the master of ceremonies. He started by introducing the wedding party.

"At the far end is Melville's best man and flying instructor," Wilbur announced. He motioned for me to stand. I did, with cheeks crammed full of potato salad. I concentrated on keeping my mouth closed and nodded.

Uncle Wilbur looked at Mary Ellen. "Young lady, I want you to know that this man has spent a lot of time with Melville in a tiny airplane. I don't know what they were doing but it must have been something cozy."

The crowd roared. I stifled a laugh and covered my mouth so I would not lose any food.

Wilbur finished the introductions and then proposed a few toasts. Every time I lifted my fork it was time to stand and clink glasses.

"And finally, we have a special presentation to make," Wilbur declared. I stuffed a wad of bread into my mouth. "I'd like the best man to come up and do the honours." Wilbur looked my way. I had no idea what he was talking about.

I pushed my chair back slowly and chewed madly. Wilbur reached under the podium and pulled out a bag. It looked like the one Darcy and Mimi had brought to the reception. I paced my steps to reach the podium with a mostly empty mouth.

Wilbur leaned away from the microphone. "Apparently you know what this is about," he said, handing me the bag.

I didn't have a clue. I looked into the bag. The spot landing trophy was staring up at me. I lifted it out. A buzz went through the crowd. There was a note taped to the bottom of the trophy. I recognized Leanne's handwriting. "Winner of the first annual Flying Circus Spot Landing Contest, Melville Passmore." Underneath she had written, "He was the only one to hit the line."

I bent to the microphone, "Thank you, Uncle Wilbur." I held up the trophy. "This is something to add to this already exciting day." I glanced at Melville seated nearby. He looked puzzled. "Earlier today, Melville Passmore entered a spot landing contest with his airplane at the Circus Airport." Melville's face began to lose colour. He probably thought that I was going to say something about his hard landing. I did.

"This was not an easy competition. The pilots approached the runway at 75 mph. They had to land their main wheels on a line that was only one foot wide. There were over 30 entries. It is my pleasure to announce that Melville Passmore hit the line on his first and only try. He has been declared the first place winner of the contest. Congratulations Melville!"

The crowd clapped, cheered and whistled. Melville's face turned from despair to surprise. He started to get up but I didn't want him to start talking about the landing. I placed the trophy in front of him with one hand and pressed him back into his seat with the other. "Way to go, Ace," I said. We shook hands and I returned to my seat.

Uncle Wilbur stepped up to the microphone. "It is now time to invite the new Mr. and Mrs. Passmore to take to the floor for the first dance."

The music started. Mary Ellen and Melville walked onto the floor and held each other. Cameras flashed and people applauded. I watched from the head table while shamelessly shoveling more food into my face. The round farmer and his new wife danced very well together.

The master of ceremonies announced that the rest of the wedding party should join them. Porcia jumped up beside me. She was losing her shyness. "That's us," she declared holding out a muscled arm.

"My pleasure," I gargled. I had a mouthful of beef and gravy.

I stood up. Portia kicked off her running shoes, grabbed my arm and towed me onto the dance floor. She swung me around the room with surprising strength. It took me the whole number to chew down the leathery piece of dairy cow.

The song ended but she hung on to me for the next number. The disc jockey obliged by sliding straight into a polka. Uncle Wilbur invited everyone to join in. Most of them did.

Porcia pumped us through the growing crowd using me as a battering ram when necessary.

"Thank you, Portia," I said at the end of the song. "I'm going back to finish my supper."

She stuck out her lower lip in a pout. I pulled away. She followed.

We both sat down at the table. Portia leaned on an elbow and watched while I dug into some cold mashed potatoes and gravy. The DJ played a rocking Billy-Ray Cyrus tune.

Portia straightened up as soon as the forkful hit my mouth. "Dance

I was trying not to spray food on this nice-looking lady.

with me now?" she asked. "That's my most favourite song!"

I shook my head back and forth and refilled my fork. I kept my mouth full during the entire number. The chicken dance came on next.

Portia jumped up and pulled on my arm. "This is the best!" she declared. "We have to dance!"

I pointed to my full mouth.

"You don't have to sing," she said, still pulling, "just wiggle."

I was about to give in when I spotted Melville steering a young woman toward us. The lady was short like Melville but less round. She looked about my age. She was dressed casually but her clothes were definitely not barn wear. Portia saw them and let go of my arm.

"I want you to meet Mrs. Thomas," Melville yelled excitedly.

I leaned across the table to accept the lady's handshake.

"Pleased to meet you," the woman said pleasantly.

She was pretty in a wholesome way. I pointed to my bulging cheeks in reply. She smiled and then greeted Portia.

Melville looked at me. "You two are my very favourite teachers," he declared. "I gotta run." He flashed me a knowing smile and then scooted back to the dance floor.

Portia huffed off in a different direction.

"Melville mentioned that you are his flying instructor," Mrs. Thomas said. Her voice was clear and friendly but firm.

I stopped chewing long enough to nod.

"I wanted to meet you," she continued, "because I thought it would take a special person to teach Melville how to fly."

I forced down as much mouth contents as I could. "Yeth," I replied stupidly. I was trying not to spray food on this nice-looking lady, "Watt did you teash him?"

"Melville was in my Grade 3-4 class but I didn't really teach him anything. I discovered that he had to learn things for himself."

This woman was obviously not another doting farm wife. I stopped chewing and swallowed the rest of my mouthful.

"I discovered the same thing," I said with a cough.

Mrs. Thomas's pleasant teacher's face clouded slightly. "I think it would be difficult to learn flying on your own."

"Not really," I said, trying to sound authoritative. I motioned to the empty chair beside me. "Would you like to sit down?"

"No, thank you," she replied. "I shouldn't keep you from your meal."

She had a soft, round face and large beautiful eyes. She held my attention with a warm but penetrating gaze. I could imagine her controlling a whole classroom of kids with that same steady look.

I suddenly wasn't hungry anymore. I scanned the room to see if a Mr. Thomas was charging across the floor. I wiped my mouth with a serviette. "Would you like to dance, Mrs. Thomas?"

She blushed a little and smiled some more. "You finish your supper," she said. "Besides, I shouldn't steal you from your dance partner."

"Actually, I was hungry but I took too much food and now I can't eat it all," I blurted out. "I'd rather not sit here by myself. Please, sit down or dance with me."

Her blush turned to a heavy pink but she was still smiling. "Call me Carol, and yes, I'd like to dance."

I steered Carol Thomas around the dance floor during a slow song. She held me at a respectable distance.

"Learning to fly wasn't too difficult for Melville," I said. "It related nicely to operating farm machinery. I let him teach me how to teach him."

She watched my face as I talked.

"It must have worked but isn't there math involved in subjects like navigation?" she asked.

"Yes, and Melville has trouble with numbers but he can do proportions. He knows if it takes him so many minutes to fly one quarter of the way, then his estimated time enroute and fuel consumed is three more of those same quarters."

Her eyes lit up. "I found the same thing," she said enthusiastically. "It wasn't until I visited the Passmore farm that I realized how proportions worked for Melville. He showed me how he kept track of the herd, their feed and their milk."

I shook my head knowingly as we danced. "I wish I'd discovered that sooner. I wasted a lot of our time and his money before we were on the same wavelength."

"You weren't the only one," she replied. "The other teachers in the school had trouble grasping the idea of Melville learning his own way."

I dared a change of subject. "If you don't mind my asking, is there a Mr. Thomas?"

"I don't mind," she blushed. "Mr. Thomas is long gone."

So is he dead or what? I asked myself.

"I'm separated from my spouse as well," I said.

She gave me another soft smile. "I know."

I leaned back without letting her go. "How come everyone here knows everything about me and I don't know anyone?"

Her smile widened, "Welcome to the country."

We danced and talked through three songs. Then a shift to hard rock music drove us from the floor.

"I was sitting with parents of kids that I have taught," she said. "Would you like to join us?"

"Yes, I would."

I was introduced to six sets of country parents.

"We met you in the receiving line," the first man said.

"It was amazing that Melville won that trophy," his wife added.

"Yes, it was," I replied, then I smiled, "but he had a good instructor."

"Whooee," one of the other husbands hooted. "Will you listen to him? Next thing he'll be telling us he was flying the plane."

"No," I laughed, "Melville did it on his own. He's a good pilot."

After the introductions, the conversation turned to the wedding and the folks at the reception. I wasn't going to say anything but this group expected otherwise.

"What did you think of the wedding?" one lady asked me.

"I thought Mary Ellen looked very beautiful," I offered.

"Yes!" another lady exclaimed, "and she did so well."

Carol leaned my way and said softly, "Mary Ellen is deaf."

"You're kidding!" I blurted out in surprise.

"You didn't know?" the woman across from us exclaimed. "Well, I guess you wouldn't. That little girl is wonderful. She reads lips. Her dad paced her down the aisle to the music. She watched the minister to know when to speak and she knew her lines perfectly."

"That's why they curved the head table," the first lady said, pointing to the end of the hall, "so Mary Ellen could read the lips of the people in the wedding party."

The talk turned to the reception. I learned that only close friends and relatives were invited to the wedding ceremony because of the small church but the reception was wide open to the whole community.

"If it's not done like that," a middle-aged mother said, "sure as shootin' someone would be forgot. Then there'd be hell to pay. This way, anyone who wants to come, can."

I was told that the reception doesn't cost the bride and groom or their parents anything. Each family attending contributes food. The profits from the cash bar cover expenses like the disc jockey.

"It's as good an excuse as any for a community party," one man cheered. Then he swigged more beer.

The music slowed. Carol looked my way.

"Carol, would you like to dance?"

"Yes, thank you."

She let me hold her closer but there was still daylight between us.

"Knowing about Mary Ellen's deafness makes the wedding ceremony extra special," I said. "Thanks for mentioning it."

"You're welcome. Right now Melville is guiding her on the dance floor to music that she can't hear."

I looked over her shoulder. The newlyweds were dancing nearby. "They make a good couple," I said.

"I agree."

At eleven o'clock, the bride and groom said their "goodbyes" to everyone. Mary Ellen tossed her bouquet. Carol stayed out of range. Portia caught it.

"It's time that this little school teacher headed home," Carol said to me. She offered a handshake. "Thank you for the conversation and the dancing."

"Thank you!" I said shaking her hand. "Let me help you with your coat."

We retrieved her ski jacket from the cloakroom. I held it for her while trying to think of a good way to ask for her phone number. "Do you have far to go?" I inquired.

“A little ways,” she replied. “I live on this side of Derry but I have my own car. How about you?” She shrugged the rest of the way into her coat.

Damn, I said to myself. I hadn’t thought about getting home. My face turned red. Carol noticed it.

“Did I say something wrong?”

“No, not at all,” I replied sheepishly. “I know where I live, but not how I’m going to get there.”

I explained how Melville and I had flown to his place and driven in his car from there.

“Can I give you a ride back to your plane?” Carol offered, zipping up her jacket.

“Actually, that won’t help. Passmore’s landing strip is not lit so I can’t fly out of there until morning.”

Carol smiled. “So you need a ride home and then a ride to Passmore’s in the morning.”

I felt like an idiot. “You don’t want to do that,” I sighed. “I live 40 minutes from here in the wrong direction for you. Then you’d have to drive all the way home and, in a few hours, drive all the way back to take me to Passmore’s.”

She watched my eyes. “Well, this country girl doesn’t sleep with men she has just met, so I’m not inviting you to my place and I’m not staying overnight at yours.”

Now we were both blushing.

“You have to believe me,” I moaned. “This is not a setup. I really am this dumb. Melville and I planned our transportation all the way to this reception without thinking of afterward.”

I couldn’t believe that I was trying to convince this pretty, clever, unattached female that I was stupid. At least she was still smiling.

She placed a hand on my arm. “I like to drive,” she said, “and tomorrow is a day off for me. Unless you have a better alternative, I’d be happy to give you a ride home.”

“I’d appreciate it.”

“Good. Where’s your coat?”

“I don’t have one.”

“Then we’d better put the top up.”

Chapter Fourteen

The fast lane

Carol and I walked out of the community hall into a chilly spring night. Her car was a white MGB roadster parked near the back of the gravel lot. In the light of an old post lamp the car looked driven hard and put away wet. The body was dented, the paint was scratched and the chrome bumpers were slightly askew. The car did not fit the image of a country schoolteacher.

"I don't see many of these around anymore," I said to make conversation. "What year is it?"

"It depends on which part. It began as a 1972 model but the top has been replaced three times, the engine twice and the transmission once. The body has been rebuilt but it needs it again. I've given up on the upholstery."

The MG's top was down and a layer of dew covered the interior.

"I'll dig out a towel for your seat," Carol offered.

She reached into the driver's door pouch. I walked around to the other side of the car. She leaned over and handed me a cloth. I smeared the dampness around the cracked leather and handed it back. Carol wiped both sides of the windshield and her seat and then tucked the wet rag inside the door.

"The top is easy to raise," she said. "Just follow what I do."

We swung the top up and clamped it to the windshield frame. Carol passed me a side window from behind the seats. I looked at how she was fastening hers and tried the reverse on my side. I got it on but it didn't look right. Carol climbed in and started the engine.

Five minutes later we were blasting down a country road. I hung onto the passenger handle on the dashboard. The cool dampness from the seat seeped through my clothes to my backside. The instrument lights were

"How about a little low flying?" she shouted.

out so I could not see the speedometer but the noise indicated we were going fast. The wind shrieked through my side window frame and the small engine revved at a high pitch. I stuck my free hand under an armpit for warmth.

Carol diddled something in the middle of the panel. My left foot heated up immediately. Soon it was burning. I drew both feet back but then I couldn't see over my knees. I shuffled and squirmed until I found a position where I could see ahead without setting fire to my shoes.

"Is that better?" she called out.

"Much!"

"How about a little low flying?" she shouted.

"What do you mean?" I yelled back.

"Watch!"

The hydro poles flickered past in the headlights. An intersection with a four-way stop appeared ahead.

"There's nobody coming," Carol declared. "Hang on!"

She accelerated and blew through the intersection. The crown on the crossing road launched us into the air. The engine revved briefly and then the car smacked back onto the road. There was a loud bang, a clatter and then the exhaust noise changed to a roar.

"Rear axle chopped off the muffler again!" Carol shouted. "It must be your extra weight."

"Sorry," I yelled.

"Don't worry. I'm on muffler guarantee number five. Now we can go faster."

The roar increased.

I didn't try any more conversation. I watched Carol drive. It was less frightening than looking ahead. Her seat was pulled all the way forward so she could reach the pedals. Behind her was more room than in front. She was sitting up straight with her arms bent to the steering wheel. The drafts bounced her hair around. She was grinning.

Carol downshifted and braked hard when I indicated that my driveway was coming up. She turned in, stopped in front of the barn and shut off the engine. My ears were ringing and my left shoe was smoldering. The rest of my body was numb with cold.

Lady, my German shepherd, approached the strange car cautiously in the glow of the yard light. She planted her front paws on the driver's door to see in. Carol slid her side window open a few inches.

"Nice boy. How are you doing? Are you a good dog?"

Lady whined a reply.

I translated. "She said, 'Did you bring my shiftless owner home to feed me?'"

At the sound of my voice Lady bounced around to my side of the car. I opened my door so she wouldn't scratch it. She plopped her front half onto my lap and licked my face. Carol offered her a pat. She sniffed. Carol rubbed her ears. The dog tried to crawl across me to get to the driver's side.

"No Lady, get down," I said.

She did.

"Nice dog," Carol said.

"She must like you," I replied. "My ex-wife trained her to bite other women."

"I don't believe you."

"You haven't met my ex-wife."

She changed the subject. "What time should I be here to pick you up in the morning?"

"The airplane doesn't have to be back to the flying school until ten o'clock. Would you like to go for a short airplane ride before I head to Circus?"

A frown flashed across her face. She hesitated and then smiled. "That would be great."

I worked out the timing. "Thirty minutes to Passmores, 30 minutes to ready the airplane, a 30-minute sightseeing flight and 30 minutes to Circus. Can you pick me up here by eight o'clock?"

"I'll be here."

The dog and I climbed out my side of the car. "Thanks for the ride," I said, closing the door.

"Thanks for the company. It was a nice evening."

The roar of the MGB cut off any further thoughts or conversation as Carol started the engine. Lady scooted behind me. Carol backed out of the driveway and waved. I did too. She roared off.

Chapter Fifteen

Low and slow

Lady and I played catch outside with a Frisbee while I waited for my ride the next morning. It was crisp and cool but a clear sky promised a warmer day.

I stood in the damp grass sorting out my thoughts about the modest but capable Carol Thomas. I had not been looking for a relationship. Suddenly finding someone interesting was a surprise.

Don't waste your thoughts, I said to myself. Carol met you with your mouth so crammed with free food that you couldn't talk but tried to anyway. She left you needing someone to give you a ride because you couldn't plan half a day ahead. Forget about a relationship. Besides, you've been enjoying the independence of being single. You are free to focus on the air service, free to work long hours, and free to have nobody to share your life with.

The dog snapped me out of my thoughts with one sharp bark. She was waiting for me to continue our play. I spun the plastic disk across the yard. Lady sat as usual and watched it land. Then she trotted over, picked it up and was returning it when she stopped. She turned her head and pointed her ears up the road. Several seconds went by before I could hear the unmuffled sound of a small-bore engine revved to full chat. The noise grew louder. Then it suddenly screamed as Carol downshifted her MGB. The white car appeared from beside the roadside barn with its nose dipped under hard braking. The top was down.

Lady dropped the Frisbee and ran toward the driveway, her tail wagging madly. Carol turned in, killed the engine and coasted to a stop. The dog planted her front paws on the driver-side door.

"How are you doing, girl?" Carol said to her, rubbing her ears. "Such a good dog."

I walked toward the car. “Lady, get down,” I called out.

The dog turned to gauge my seriousness. Carol stopped petting her. Lady dropped her front feet to the ground.

“Good morning to you too,” Carol smiled from her driver’s seat.

She looked different. She was wearing the same old jacket but her face was more radiant. It must have been the cool air or early light.

“Good morning,” I replied, walking up to the car. “Stirling Moss, I presume?”

She tilted her head back and laughed. “Lynn St. James,” she answered, naming a female race car driver.

“Of course. Thanks for coming.”

“My pleasure.”

“I’m ready to go,” I said.

“Top up or down?”

“Down,” I replied tugging at my heavy sweater.

“OK, hop in.”

I turned to Lady. “You stay. That’s a good girl.”

The dog’s ears drooped and she sat down.

I walked to the other side of the MGB and climbed in.

“I think she wants to come with us,” Carol said.

“It’s an act. She doesn’t like getting into cars,” I replied. “She was dropped off by one. She wants us to stay and play.” I called out to the dog. “You guard the house.”

Lady barked her displeasure.

“Is that back talk?”

I shrugged. “She’s a lady.”

Carol laughed and then started the car. On the road she wound up the engine through all four gears. I leaned over to check the speedometer. It read “0”. I looked at Carol. She smiled but kept her eyes on the road. Her face glowed pink in the chilly air. I could see that she was wearing a little more make-up. I took that as a good sign for a single guy riding with a pretty girl. I wondered what I might do to impress this hot-shoe country schoolteacher during an airplane ride.

The Citabria was an aerobatic trainer. It could twist and turn like a sports car. I could also make it flip, tumble, loop and roll but I decided on something different.

We made good time to the Passmore farm. Carol parked behind the lean-to hangar at the landing strip. We walked around to the open side.

“There you go,” I gestured, “a Champion Citabria.”

She walked up to the right side ahead of the wing. “It’s not what I expected,” she said.

I leaned behind her and unlatched the door. I caught a faint whiff of perfume. Another good sign.

"Walk around the strut and you can see inside," I offered. "I'm going to undo the tie-downs and then I'll ask you to help me push it out."

I did a pre-flight inspection, untying the ropes as I went.

"Have you flown in a small airplane before?" I asked.

"I thought I had, but not this small."

"It's fun; like flying in a sports car."

We pushed the airplane outside. I had Carol climb into the rear seat and showed her how to work the four-point aerobatic harness.

"This stick, that throttle lever and those pedals are duplicates of what I have up front," I explained. "They're for training." I climbed into the pilot seat and fastened my belts. "You'll feel like you're in a hole back there," I added, "until we're airborne and flying level."

"I'm fine," she replied.

I started the engine and completed some checks without explaining anything. I wanted to use our time to fly, not to teach. I taxied to the beginning of the grass runway and stopped.

"I'm going to rev the engine to check the systems and then we'll be taking off."

"OK."

I did the run-up check and looked for traffic. The runway was clear. The cows must have been in a different field.

"All set?" I called out.

"I'm ready," Carol replied.

I advanced the throttle but not quite all the way. The Citabria accelerated slowly as it rumbled along in the grass. I held the control stick in the middle. The airplane bounced into the air in its three-point stance. I eased the nose down slightly to gain speed. We cleared the wires at the road. I reduced the power leaving enough to slowly climb. We were flying at 70 mph.

I turned to look at Carol. She was looking at me.

"Are you OK?"

"So far, so good," she replied.

I leveled off at 500 feet and throttled back to 1800 rpm. The Citabria purred along.

The sun behind us lit up the rolling farmland. I banked the airplane gently to fly over the community centre. I pointed down.

"Yes, I see it," Carol said.

"Where is your school?" I asked

She looked down at the roads, hesitated and then pointed to the west. "Over there, I think."

I turned in that direction. It looked like we were suspended in the cool, smooth air as the countryside slowly rolled by underneath. It was a peaceful scene. This early on a Sunday morning there were no cars on the roads or tractors in the fields.

I felt Carol touch my shoulder. "This is beautiful," she exclaimed. "I never imagined it would be like this. How fast are we going?"

"Seventy miles per hour," I said.

"It seems like twenty-five," she replied.

A few minutes later she touched me again. I turned my head. "The school's over there," she said, pointing one concession road to the right.

I banked the airplane gently. A few minutes later we were flying over the small country school.

I looked back at Carol. She was looking ahead, not down. "No classes today," I announced.

She smiled and nodded her agreement. "May I try flying?" she asked.

"Certainly. Hold your right hand gently on the stick and rest your feet on the pedals."

I spent the next 30 minutes talking Carol through the basic control movements of the airplane. I mentally kicked myself for not recognizing that she would be more interested in flying than sightseeing. She quickly developed a gentle touch on the stick.

I gave her a series of turns that took us back to the Passmore place. "I'll take over control now," I said pointing down at the landing strip.

"OK. Thank you very much."

I eased the Citabria around, lined up for a landing, reduced the power and glided in for a smooth touchdown. I stopped beside the hangar and shut down the engine.

"That was wonderful," Carol declared. "I didn't know flying could be so calm and so... majestic."

"I'm glad you liked it," I said, smiling to myself. It sounded like I had scored big points with the slow flight.

"I'll get out first," I said to Carol, "and then I can give you a hand."

"OK."

I opened the door, undid my belts and climbed out. When I turned around to help Carol, she already had her harness off and was leaning forward. I slid my hands under her arms. "Hang on," I said.

She gripped my shoulders and stepped into my grasp. I swung her around onto the ground, getting a nice hug in the process. I held her for another moment. Her eyes flared with a touch of distress. I released her. We stood face-to-face. Her smile returned.

"Thank you for letting me fly," she said. "That's the first time I've been in an airplane without getting motion sickness."

Chapter Sixteen

Darcy 2, Billings 0

Monday morning Buzz Billings called the police and reported that the Super Cub had been stolen. A constable was dispatched to investigate. He wrote down the particulars.

"When did this happen, Mr. Billings?"

"Friday evening."

"And you're just reporting it now?"

"I didn't work over the weekend."

"Does the control tower have a record of the aircraft's departure?"

"It was tied onto a trailer with its wings off."

"So someone hitched up the trailer and drove away?"

"It was in the locked hangar."

"Any sign of a forced entry?"

"Yes."

Billings showed the officer where the hangar door had been pried open. He didn't mention the fire department.

"Any idea who might have stolen it?"

Billings figured that Darcy had taken the Cub but he didn't want the police to find it. He wanted to claim the loss on his insurance.

"No idea at all," the aircraft dealer lied.

Monday afternoon, Billings reported the theft to his insurance broker. The agent asked Buzz to fax the information about the airplane and said that he'd check the policy.

Later he returned the call. "Buzz, your hangar policy covers aircraft named on it and additions that are reported and approved by us in writing," the agent said. "We have no record of a request to add a Super Cub to your policy."

"Are you telling me that I'm paying you insurance premiums for nothing?" the salesman barked.

"I'm telling you that you choose the lowest premium available which only covers named aircraft."

"Blast you thieving insurance people!" Billings slammed down the phone.

On Tuesday morning, Billings called the police again. He reported that someone had tried to burn down his hangar over the weekend. The same officer arrived to take his statement.

"When did this happen, Mr. Billings?"

"Friday evening."

"And you're just reporting it now?"

"I wasn't here over the weekend."

"I don't recall seeing evidence of fire damage when I was here yesterday," the constable said.

"Check with the fire department," Billings replied. "They were here."

The policeman checked with the firemen. The airport incident had been written up as a false alarm. They had not found any fire.

On Tuesday afternoon, Billings called his insurance broker again. He wanted to claim fire damage on his hangar policy. The agent said he'd look into it.

The agent called the company's claims manager who in turn connected with an insurance adjuster. The adjuster drove to Billings Aviation and introduced himself to Buzz. Billings showed him the damage to the roll-up door where the fire department had gained entry.

"Looks like your $1,000 deductible will cover it," the adjuster replied. "Is there any other damage?"

"No."

"Do you still what to make a claim?"

"I've been an insurance customer for a long time," Billings growled.

"Yes, I saw your file," the adjuster replied, "and not a good risk much of that time."

Billings glared at him. "Are you threatening me?"

"No sir," the guy answered quickly, "but you are threatening your insurance coverage when you make nuisance claims."

"Get out!"

On Wednesday The Flying Circus received a registered letter from the federal government. It contained the authority to establish an aerial advertising business at the Circus Airport. It was the completion of step one in the bureaucratic red tape. We were now allowed to begin red tape step number two, an operating certificate application for aerial advertising. Henry sent it to the government regional office that same day via courier.

On Thursday, Darcy flew the repaired Super Cub to Circus. I walked outside as he taxied onto our ramp and shut down. I stood there with my mouth open.

"You don't look any smarter with your mouth hanging like that," the wisecracking mechanic said. He climbed out of the front seat.

"Darcy, that is the ugliest airplane I have ever seen!"

The Cub wore the bright yellow factory paint on the left wing, fuselage and tail. The right wing was coloured a dull royal blue.

"Yeah, isn't it great! I thought you'd like it. You'll attract lots of attention when you're towing banners."

"I didn't think the replacement wing would be a different colour," I moaned.

He grinned. "I believe you."

"Why didn't you paint it to match?"

"I learned in pre-school that mixing blue and yellow paint makes green. Same with aircraft dope."

"Isn't that blue fabric old and rotten?"

"Old yes, rotten, not yet. When it is, we'll recover it. Is the coffee on in the office?"

"Yes."

"Who made it?"

"Leanne."

He walked past me. "Close your mouth and save some oxygen for the rest of us."

One of Darcy's men arrived in the old Fargo pick-up towing the empty airplane trailer. Henry returned from flying with a student. I took that Cherokee up with another customer. Darcy, his helper and Henry removed the wings from Melville's TriPacer while I was flying.

I returned in time to see Darcy start the wingless TriPacer's engine. He drove the fuselage onto the trailer with the nosewheel and two dollies for landing gear. The two mechanics and Henry anchored it and then tied the wings and struts alongside. They came into the office for a coffee when they were done. I joined them.

"I didn't know you flew taildraggers until you arrived in the Super Cub," I said to Darcy.

"I do now."

"Have you done any banner towing?" Henry asked.

Darcy shook his head negatively and sipped his coffee.

"Too bad. Inspector Kennedy called this morning," Henry continued.

"He's rejecting our application for aerial advertising. Our chief pilot here has no towing experience. We have to find someone who does."

Darcy swallowed. "I know someone," he said. "You know him too."

"Who?" we both asked.

"Ziggy Burns.'

Darcy drove the wingless TriPacer onto the trailer with two dollies for the main gear.

Chapter Seventeen

Ziggy

Ziggy Burns was a marvel and a mystery. We had hired him once before but we still knew nothing about him. He liked it that way. I punched in his phone number.

"Burns," he answered.

"Hi, Ziggy? I'm calling from The Flying Circus. Darcy Phillips said you might teach us banner towing."

"Thursday."

"Ah, Thursday would be..."

He had hung up.

"...good."

Ziggy arrived at the airport in his ancient Diesel Rabbit. I watched as the battered car rattled into our parking lot and coughed to a stop. The little man stepped out. He looked destitute. His bare feet wallowed in oversized shoes that were held together with duck tape, his washed-out blue jeans were worn through in spots and his faded plaid flannel shirt was semi-covered with a moth-eaten grey cardigan.

Leanne was standing beside me. "How old do you suppose he is?" she asked.

"Somewhere between thirty and fifty," I replied.

Our receptionist smiled. "The first time I met him, I wanted to take him home. The man needs to be properly fed and clothed."

"He's cheapskate enough; he would have gone with you."

Ziggy dressed poorly but he knew everything about everything and missed nothing. In one day, he taught Henry and me how to tow banners.

He showed us how to organize and clip together the letters efficiently.

Ziggy told us to rig the loop of rope between the two poles.

"Make all messages read to the right," he said.

"Why right?" I asked.

Ziggy liked to economize on words. He thought people should accept what he said. Explanations were a waste of vocabulary. Besides, professional pilots should be able to figure some things out for themselves.

"Because the recommended flight pattern around Niagara Falls is clockwise," he sighed.

"Why is that?"

Ziggy frowned. His left leg started to shake. "Am I correct or not?"

"Yes."

"Then we'll move on."

Ziggy watched and commented as Henry and I clipped a short message together. We rolled it up and loaded it into the back of Henry's Pinto along with the pick-up poles, stands and lead rope. The three of us drove out to the infield grass south of Runway 24. Ziggy told us to place the stands on the ground 20 feet apart perpendicular to the wind. Then he had us lay out a 200-foot rope from between the stands toward the southwest. We attached the banner by its lead mast to the far end of the rope and rolled out the message away from the stands at a slight angle to the wind.

Ziggy stood in the grass and watched. He looked like a small version of Jack Benny. His right arm crossed his skinny chest and held his left elbow. His left hand was stuck to the side of his face. His expression showed borderline impatience.

"Now both of you walk the length of the banner checking for problems," he said.

"What are we looking for?" I asked.

"Twisted straps, broken rods, ripped letters and correct spelling."

I felt he was treating us like children. "But we just put this thing together. We didn't use broken rods, ripped letters or wrong spelling."

Henry kept his head down and inspected the banner.

"Suit yourself," Ziggy replied. His leg was shaking again. "Check it here or change it in the air. It's your choice."

I followed Henry. We didn't find anything amiss.

"It looks good to me," I declared with a touch of sarcasm.

Ziggy bent over the third letter. "This strap has been connected backward to the clip on the rod. That shortens it."

Henry and I looked where he was pointing.

"The shorter strap will take the load of the six other straps until it breaks."

Henry bent down and re-attached the strap.

Ziggy walked to another letter. "One strap here is twisted; same problem, same result."

I crouched down, fixed it and stood up. Ziggy hadn't moved.

"Is that it?" I asked.

One hand went to his elbow and the other to his face. "I don't know. I haven't looked any further."

Henry and I checked everything again.

The grass was still wet from heavy dew that morning. Our shoes, socks and the bottoms of our pants were soaked by the time we were done.

"Does it matter if the letters are wet?" I asked.

"No," Ziggy replied. Then he anticipated my next question. "The synthetic material doesn't absorb water."

"So we can tow banners in the rain?"

"No."

This time he let me ask the question. "Why not?"

"Because people generally don't stand outside in the rain and look for aerial advertising."

"Oh, yeah."

Next, we pieced aluminum poles into two 16-foot lengths each topped with a small red flag and a V-shaped rubber fork.

The lead rope was looped at the near end. We picked up the loop with the fork on the poles and lifted it skyward. Then we guided the wobbling poles into the stands. The result was a loop of rope strung between the top of the two poles, trailing to the ground and running to the banner.

"Who's first to fly the pick-up?" Ziggy asked.

Henry and I pointed to each other.

"OK, paper, rock, scissors on three," Ziggy said. "One, two, three."

I did rock; Henry's open palm signaled paper.

Ziggy pointed to Henry. "You won, you're first."

Henry pointed to me. "No, I won, he goes first."

Chapter Eighteen

Hooked

Ziggy's voice boomed loud and clear in my headset, "Toss it now!" I changed hands on the airplane's control stick and gathered up the three-pound grappling hook and its 50 feet of cable from my lap.

"Toss it, don't throw it!" he barked.

Ziggy was sitting behind me in the cramped cockpit of the Super Cub. He had to bark to be heard over the wind noise blasting through the open door on the right side.

The other end of the wire cable trailed out the door. It was clipped to a release mechanism under the airplane's tail. I held my handful of hook and cable into the slipstream, aimed behind the wing strut and tossed.

"Now skid the airplane to the right," Ziggy yelled. "The hook should be trailing below and behind us."

I pressed on the right rudder pedal and turned in my seat to look back. I leaned my head into the slipstream and glimpsed the yellow hook swinging on the cable. Then the air blast ripped off my headset and sent my hat and sunglasses spinning into oblivion.

"How's the cable?" Ziggy shouted.

I was more interested in the lost earphones than the hook. I looked at him. He was holding my headset which he had caught with his right hand. His left hand was motioning for me to look out the door.

It was typical Ziggy: lesson learned, move on. I waved a thumbs-up.

"Close the door!" he barked.

I clamped the control stick between my knees, reached up for the top half of the door and unlatched it from the underside of the wing. I held it with my left hand and swung the bottom half of the door up with my right, fitted them together and closed the latch.

Ziggy handed me the headset. It was still plugged in.

"Toss it, don't throw it!"

"Call the control tower," he ordered.

"Circus Tower, Charlie Uniform Bravo is downwind for the banner pick-up."

"Charlie Uniform Bravo is cleared low and over the infield south of Runway 24, wind 230 five to ten."

"Uniform Bravo."

I recognized the controller's voice. It was Barry McDay.

Barry came on the frequency again. "I bet five dollars that you miss it first try."

I ignored him, took a deep breath and reduced the power on the Cub's engine. Then I commenced a descending turn to the left, holding the bank angle until we were flying parallel to the active runway.

I could see the two red flags well ahead.

"Remember," Ziggy warned, "the hook trails only 10 to 20 feet below the tail."

"Better too high than too low?"

"Better to be right on," the tough little instructor replied. It was another typical Ziggy response. He could not understand people who didn't do things right the first time.

I wiggled up in my seat and concentrated on my target. Now I could see the poles and the rope strung between them. It looked like only luck could make a hook swinging on a 50-foot cable catch 20 feet of rope sagging 12 feet off the ground. I added power to check the Cub's descent.

"You're too high!" Ziggy snapped.

How did he know? I was in the front seat straining to look over the nose. There was no way the little man could see past my 200-pound bulk unless he was standing up. I glanced back. He was sitting calmly with his arms folded gazing out the right side window. It looked like he was counting dandelions in the grass.

"I'll bet ten dollars that you miss," Barry said over the radio.

I held the altitude and concentrated on the rope ahead.

"Still too high!" the back seat yelled.

I felt my control stick jerk forward as Ziggy shoved on his. I let the Cub drop down a few feet. We looked to be too low. If we were, the hook could snag in the grass or bounce off the ground and wrap itself around the Cub's tail.

Henry was standing off to the left beside his Pinto. He was there to watch and to reset the rig if the wind blew it down or if I knocked it over.

The poles were rushing toward me. It looked like the Cub's tires would catch the rope.

Ziggy shouted one more time, "Too high!"

"No we're not!" I hollered back. I applied full power and pulled the nose up to start a climb. Then I reached down for the tow release handle on the floor. I tensed for the tug of the hook pulling the rope from the poles and peeling the banner off the grass. If the Cub slowed too much, I was ready to pull the release.

I didn't feel anything.

"You were too high," Ziggy said. "Go around and try it again."

I let the Cub continue its climb.

"You pitched up too early," my instructor continued. "When the nose goes up, the tail goes down and the hook goes up."

I flew another circuit. I was determined to catch the rope on the next pass. It was the first time a banner pick-up had been attempted at the Circus Airport. I knew I was being watched by staff from the airport office, the control tower and the rival flying club.

"Charlie Uniform Bravo is downwind for the banner pick-up."

"Charlie Uniform Bravo is cleared low and over south of Runway 24," Barry replied, "wind 230 at ten."

"Uniform Bravo."

I reduced the power and set up another approach. Flaps at two notches and airspeed at 75 mph. I lined up between the poles and continued descending.

"Double or nothing?" Barry asked over the radio. I could hear the smirk in his voice.

I didn't reply.

"The airplane tires will not catch the rope," Ziggy said, "if it does not appear above the horizon in the windshield as we approach."

It was good advice. I eased the Cub down until the rope looked to be just below the horizon. I was sure we were too low but I ignored the feeling and concentrated on keeping the airplane steady. Ziggy said nothing. I continued past the point where I had pulled up the last time. The rope disappeared under the nose. I waited one more second.

"Now!" Ziggy shouted.

I shoved the throttle forward, pulled the nose up and moved my left hand down to the release lever. The Cub started to climb and then slowed. We had snagged something.

"Lower the nose!" Ziggy shouted. He shoved on his stick. "Maintain 70 mph no matter what!"

I pushed the airplane's nose toward level. The airspeed needle flickered just below 70 but I could feel the drag decreasing. The Cub began to climb again.

"It looks like a clean pick-up," Barry announced in my headset, "but I can't read it until you turn."

"Uniform Bravo checks, thank you."

"You're welcome."

I waited another minute to be sure we continued climbing and then banked into a gentle left turn. Ziggy and I were headed for our target market, the City of Niagara Falls not far to the southeast.

The Cub flew quite well considering it was towing a seven-foot by 75-foot banner on the end of a 200-foot rope. The control response rolling into the turn was slow but positive. The nose was riding high but normal for climbing at low speed. I started to relax and enjoy the slow ride over the country.

"Open your window and check the banner in the turn," Ziggy ordered.

"What am I looking for?"

"Nothing: no twists, no snags or no banner."

I flew with my left hand, held the headset with my right, slid open the window, stuck out my head and looked back.

"It's fine."

"Good. Now level off and set up a 65-mph cruise."

I rolled the Cub out of the turn, lowered the nose and reduced the power. The airplane settled into level flight with just 2250 rpm.

"Why do we fly so slow?"

"Were the letters flapping?"

"Yes."

"How long before a flag shreds in a 65-mph wind?"

"So, the slower the better."

"You're catching on."

"Then why not 60 mph?"

"Try it."

I did but I needed 2350 rpm to hold altitude. "Too much drag."

"Right. Now do a pre-landing check."

I called out the check. "Carb heat on, engine instruments in the green, primer locked, mixture full rich, magnetos both on, fuel on the left tank, quantity good, seat belts on, carb heat off."

As soon as I had pushed the carb heat knob in, the engine failed. I looked down and saw that Ziggy had pulled the throttle back to idle.

"Wrong reaction," he shouted. "Airspeed, airspeed, airspeed!"

The speed indicator was winding rapidly back. The banner was stopping the powerless Cub cold. I felt Ziggy shove his stick forward.

"Practice engine failure," he declared. "Where would you land?"

I held the nose down and looked at the ground.

"This vineyard right underneath us," I replied smartly.

"You'd wreck the airplane, the banner and maybe the pilot."

"But we can't glide anywhere with the banner!"

"Correct." He moved the throttle forward to restore the power. "That's why we have the release. You save the banner by dropping it and save your neck by gliding further without it."

I could feel the blood of embarrassment rushing to my head.

"Climb back up and then recheck the banner."

"Yes, sir."

I regained our altitude and checked the banner, closing the window smartly when I did. I trimmed the airplane level and took a deep breath. The back seat stayed quiet but not for long. I looked down for a moment.

"Do you see that traffic?" Ziggy suddenly yelled.

My head jerked up and the hairs on the back of my neck snapped to attention. The cold fear of impending doom washed over me. I couldn't see any traffic.

"No, where?" I shouted.

"Anywhere," Ziggy answered calmly. "Keep looking around for traffic. You'll never get out of anybody's way in a hurry towing a banner. Did you call clear of the control zone?"

He knew I hadn't. I gave my heart a chance to calm down.

"Circus Tower, Charlie Uniform Bravo is clear of your zone to the southeast level at two thousand two hundred feet."

"Charlie Uniform Bravo, roger," Barry replied. "I have a question before you go."

"Shoot."

"Does your banner say what I think it says?"

I smiled to myself. "What do you think it says?"

"Well, I read it backward through the binoculars. If I'm right, I can't say it on the air."

"You've got it right."

Henry and I had planned to tow a short advertisement for our banner business during this training but Don Hitchcock had requested something else. The banner was a message for his nephew congratulating him on the arrival of his new son. The nephew was Richard Peter Hitchcock III. The baby was named Richard Peter Hitchcock IV.

The banner read: "RICHARD HAS A SMALL DICK".

Chapter Nineteen

An ill wind

Inspector Kennedy seeped into our office like a bad draft. The occasion was a government base inspection for the issuing of an Aerial Advertising Operating Certificate, or not.

Kennedy and I had crossed paths several times, always with poor results for me. I called him Inspector Crusty but never to his face. He looked like a mortician. He walked with a slow glide and dressed in an ancient dark suit that hung like drapes on his lean frame. Permanent frown lines creased his sour face.

Henry had suggested that he handle this visit.

"Are you looking for a nervous breakdown?" I had asked.

"I'd worry more if he was talking to you," he had replied.

I booked myself with students for the day.

Kennedy caught my eye as he closed the door. "This inspection had better not be a waste of time," he announced.

Your time or ours? I asked myself. "Good morning, sir," I replied. "Would you like a cup of coffee?"

"I don't drink coffee."

I took that as, No thank you.

Henry was sitting at a briefing table. "Have a seat over here, sir," he offered before I could say any more.

Kennedy sat down at the table, opened his briefcase and announced to Henry, "We'll start with the paperwork."

"Which documents would you like to see?" my partner asked politely.

"Everything. Then I'll know if you know what is required."

My first student arrived. I skipped his briefing and led him straight outside to the airplane.

I returned an hour and a half later.

The desk was piled high.

Henry and Kennedy were still parked at the table in the centre of the room. It was now piled high with books and papers. Leanne sat hunkered down in her chair behind the flight desk. She was keeping her head buried in her work as if to avoid any sparks that might fly from the briefing area. My next student was waiting on the sofa beside the coffee maker.

"Our reference library hasn't changed," I heard Henry suggest.

Kennedy was thumbing through the government manuals required in the library of all air services. He marked them off his check sheet, one at a time. He didn't reply.

"These are the same books that you checked during a base inspection three months ago," Henry added.

"That was to maintain your flight training certificate," Kennedy replied firmly. "This inspection is for aerial advertising."

Henry didn't mention that Crusty had looked at the same books during our aerial charter inspection before that.

"Now I'd like to see your records for each pilot's licence, medical certificate and training."

"We're using the same pilots for banner towing that we do for flight training and charter flying," Henry said hopefully.

"Then they should be up-to-date or you won't be doing any of that either," granite face replied. "Where are they?"

I finished with my first student and quickly ushered my second one out the door.

We returned at noon. Kennedy was standing up from the briefing table when we entered the office.

"After lunch we shall inspect the aircraft and safety equipment," he said to Henry.

"Yes, sir," my partner replied.

Henry looked unhappy. I thought that he might be catching whatever made Kennedy miserable.

The deadpan inspector dropped his check sheets into his briefcase, closed it and glided out the door without acknowledging my presence.

Leanne recorded my flight and invoiced my student.

"So what's the good news?" I asked Henry.

"No news is good news, I guess," he sighed. He unfolded himself from his chair and stretched. "So far he has followed the regular base inspection format. Aerial advertising has hardly been mentioned."

"Well, thanks for this one."

"You're welcome, but you owe me."

"I know."

Henry and I ate our bag lunches in the office with Leanne.

"Inspector Kennedy is out there sitting in his car," Leanne observed.

"Is the car running?" I asked.

She stretched in her seat to see better through the window.

"I can't tell."

"If it was," Henry asked, "were you going to gas him by plugging the exhaust pipe?"

I grinned. "You took the words out of my mouth."

"Well, leave him alone. We need his signature on our operating certificate for banner towing. Then I'd be happy to help you."

I had departed with my next student when Kennedy resumed his inspection. I taught an hour of practice takeoffs and landings in the Cherokee 140 before taxiing back to the ramp. I could see Henry and the government inspector standing beside the Super Cub at the mouth of the hangar.

I debriefed my student in the office and booked him another lesson. The two men came through the door from the hangar as we were finishing. Kennedy walked by me to the briefing table. Henry followed. I gave him a questioning look. He shrugged.

I said, "Goodbye," to my student and turned my attention to the middle of the room.

"Well, I think that about covers it," Kennedy said to Henry. "I'll process your application the next time I'm back in the office and have it mailed to you." He closed his briefcase with a decisive thump and made to leave.

Henry stopped him. "Sir, I have some questions for you that should only take a few minutes," my partner said.

The miserable inspector's permanent frown deepened. He looked at his watch. "What kind of questions?"

"Aerial advertising questions."

"We have completed the aerial advertising base inspection," the older man declared.

Henry remained seated. "I was hoping you could help us with some of your aviation knowledge and experience."

Kennedy's body English bent toward the door. He looked at his watch again. "I don't have time."

My partner could be stubborn. I knew he wouldn't give in to Kennedy easily.

"You came here today to see if we were ready to fly aerial advertising, correct?"

Kennedy nodded his head in a slight positive motion. "Yes," he answered tentatively.

"Well sir, we're not ready, not until we fill in some blanks in what we know."

"Then you shouldn't have scheduled a base inspection," Kennedy answered sternly.

"You wouldn't be here to help me if I hadn't."

Henry punctuated the statement by pulling out the inspector's chair.

Kennedy sat down. He looked at his watch and said, "I only have a few minutes. I need to take that government car in for service before I return to the office."

"Thank you, sir. I appreciate your extra time." Henry's tone was genuine. "I noticed that you didn't look at our banner equipment."

"What's your question?"

"Well, the tail hook release mechanism was installed under a Supplementary Type Certificate indicating that it was engineered and certified to be safe for use on the Super Cub." Henry paused.

Kennedy sat poker faced.

Henry continued. "Is there a standard for the design, construction and maintenance of everything that attaches to the hook?"

The inspector seemed a bit relieved by the question.

"No," he replied.

"So we can attach anything to the tail and fly it?"

"I didn't say that," Kennedy snapped back.

Henry thought for a moment.

Kennedy started to rise. "If there are no..."

"There are," my partner said. "Do you have any idea how much the Super Cub's fuel consumption will increase when towing banners?"

"That's for you to know. The Department of Transport is not in the training business."

"You said that we must carry the Pilot's Operating Handbook on board but the fuel burn will be higher than the book figures."

"It's a requirement to have the Pilot's Operating Handbook in the aircraft."

"Surely we're not safe using its figures."

"I didn't say you were."

Kennedy was good at non-answers. He sounded like a politician without a personality. He studied his watch again and stood up.

"I'd like to ask a few more questions," Henry said firmly.

"I must be going," Kennedy replied, more firmly.

Henry leaned back in his chair and looked the inspector in the eye. "I can't believe a man in your position could not contribute more to aviation. Nothing you looked at here today will add to the safety of our aerial advertising flying but I endured your inspection anyway. Now you're telling us to test fly banners to determine fuel consumption. That's like spinning an airplane to see if it will recover."

Kennedy's face turned red. "That's preposterous!"

"Yes, it is!" Henry retorted. "We are the only air service in your region currently banner towing, we're the first to fly seven-foot letters and we're doing it with a new airplane. Now it's two o'clock and I'd appreciate it if you'd postpone your car's oil change and be more helpful."

Kennedy glared at my partner with a look fit for a devil.

Henry didn't flinch.

Oh, oh, I thought. Here comes the explosion. I tried to make myself smaller against the flight desk.

The now furious inspector grabbed his briefcase by its handle and yanked it off the table.

Henry kept talking. "You confirmed that we can repair our own banner equipment, which is useful, but if you've ever towed anything with an aircraft, you could save us a lot of time, money and grief on how it affects safety and performance."

My student arrived. I grabbed an aircraft logbook. "Ready when you are," I said to him hurriedly. "We'll talk about our lesson during the walkaround." I herded him outside and closed the door.

My student and I taxied for a local flight. I hadn't seen Kennedy leave yet. I spent the hour wondering if I'd return to find the propellers removed from our airplanes, padlocks on the doors and yellow crime tape skirting the premises.

There was none of that. I could see Kennedy's government car in our lot when my student taxied us to the ramp. I dreaded what might be going on inside the office. I debriefed my student in the airplane. Nobody came out of the building and no one appeared in the windows. We exited the airplane and approached the office.

"You go first," I said to my student, motioning him ahead.

He gave me a strange look and opened the door.

There were four people inside. Leanne sat smiling behind the flight desk, Henry and Kennedy were talking and laughing at the briefing table and my next student was listening to them from the couch.

"What were you two doing parked so long in the airplane?" Leanne asked me.

My brain didn't process what she said. I was looking at Inspector Kennedy leaning back in his chair with his hands clasped behind his head. He was grinning.

"Our biggest worry when we towed targets behind T-33s in the air force was not the fuel consumption," he chuckled, "it was being shot down."

Henry laughed. "Hopefully no one will be shooting at us over Niagara Falls."

Kennedy caught my eye. The grin slid off his face. He tipped his chair forward onto its four legs and spoke to Henry, "Well, if that's all, I'll take my leave." He patted his briefcase and said, "I'll go into the office first thing tomorrow and process this Operating Certificate. Do you want me to courier it to you so you have it before the weekend?"

"That would be excellent," Henry replied.

Both men stood up and shook hands.

"You've been a great help," Henry smiled. "Thanks for staying."

"I should have done that without the lecture but you know the rut we get into with these government jobs."

Henry blushed a little. "I guess so."

A different Inspector Kennedy picked up his briefcase and nodded to Leanne. "It's been a pleasure, Mrs. Rains."

"Yes, likewise, thank you," Leanne replied.

Kennedy marched smartly toward the door. He paused as he passed me. "You're lucky to be working with these people," he said.

I opened my mouth to reply but nothing came out.

Chapter Twenty

Abrevi8ions

The toughest part of our banner business was creating catchy ads without exceeding the maximum letters. The aerial towing book said the Super Cub would pull 35 large characters including spaces.

"That's in ideal conditions," Ziggy Burns had told us, "flown by a pilot who knows what he's doing." He looked at me when he said that. "First get good, then get long," he continued. "Start with no more than 25 letters and don't let your customers talk you into more than 30."

"How will we know if a banner's too long?" I asked.

The little instructor's mouth twisted into a smirk. "Crashing would be a big clue. Better to add one letter at a time over 25 and quit while you're ahead. Remember, each tow will be different."

He lost me on that one. "What do you mean?"

Ziggy frowned. "I mean each tow will be different. Are all your other flights the same?"

"No."

"Why not?"

"Things change: the weather, the load, the airplane, the destination..."

"There you go."

"But if we stick to the maximum letters, fly in good weather only, with the same airplane, from the same airport, over the same area, what will be different?"

The look on Ziggy's face darkened and his left leg started to shake but he answered me, sort of.

"Will the temperature be the same? How about wind and humidity? Are your letters going to stay in good condition? Will they always be assembled correctly? Will the Super Cub perform like new forever? Will the pilot be the same or will some be fatter and less competent?"

"OK, I get it."

The cloth banner characters weren't heavy. Ziggy had told us that the letter limit was from the drag during the pick up and towing. The message, "RICHARD HAS A SMALL DICK", was perfect. It was a catchy 24 characters including spaces but I could see it would be tricky to fit good ads into Ziggy's maximum.

Leanne had voted against flying Don Hitchcock's racy message but was overruled by her two partners. Our phone had started ringing as soon as Ziggy and I had completed one circle of Niagara Falls with the banner. Ziggy had checked Henry out towing the same message.

The response was exciting even if it wasn't all from legitimate customers. We hadn't advertised our new service. The callers had to phone around to find out our company name.

"I thought I'd heard everything," Leanne groaned. "A few perverts wanted us to tow messages from washroom stalls. I doubled our prices after listening to the first one."

"Whoa, won't that discourage real advertisers?" I asked.

"Apparently not," Leanne replied. She handed me a list. "These are prospects waiting for a call back. They have all been quoted twice what we thought the service was worth."

I followed up the first lead the next day. It was from The Dome, a theme park in Niagara Falls. The manager was a nervous little guy named Gus Drover. He wanted to advertise the 3-D African safari film being shown at their giant screen theatre. He bought an hour towing over Niagara Falls in the afternoon of the next day.

"If it brings in more people," Gus said, "I'll sign up for every weekend."

He wanted his ad to say, "GET TRAMPLED BY ELEPHANTS AT THE NIAGARA FALLS DOME". It was 51 characters. I worked with him for a long time before we got it down to 32; "GET ELEPHANT TRAMPLED AT NF DOME". It wasn't slick but it did the job. I justified the seven characters over Ziggy's limit by the fact that 24 characters had been easy to tow and this time the back seat would be empty.

The next morning Chainsaw Charlie clipped the message together while I flew with students. I arranged for Barry McDay to fly my lessons in the afternoon. At noon I drove to the infield with Chainsaw and showed him how to rig the equipment for an aerial pick-up.

The weather was good. There was the smell of spring in the warming air. The wind was calm so we unrolled the banner on the grass at an angle to the active runway. The message looked good except for the way Chainsaw had spelled, "GID".

"Charlie, the first word is spelled G-E-T."

He frowned and looked at the banner. His lips moved as he silently mouthed the words. "Well, how do you spell 'giddy'?" he asked.

"Giddy?"

"Yeah, you know, giddy-up?"

I was careful not to laugh. "Giddy-up is different. If your mom says, 'Get up,' it's G-E-T."

"Oh."

I unclipped the "I" and the "D" while Chainsaw fetched an "ET" from the hangar. I was glad I had started early. We added the letters to the message together. Then I showed him how to pick up the rope loop with the poles and set them into the stands.

The contract was for a tow from two o'clock to three. The hour was to be from the banner pick-up to the end of the towing time over the target market. This had been another spur-of-the-moment decision by Leanne when she was talking to customers. We absorbed the cost of towing the banner back to the airport and dropping it on the infield.

Chainsaw drove me to the ramp. It was 12:40, still lots of time. I planned some extra towing around the area to promote our new service.

I checked over the Super Cub and rigged the 50-foot cable from the release mechanism under the tail to the cockpit. I placed the excess cable on the pilot's seat along with the grappling hook.

I fueled the airplane, climbed in, put the cable and hook in my lap and started the engine. Then I tucked my new sunglasses into my shirt pocket and fastened my seat belt.

It felt good to be finally launching the banner service. It had been my idea and now it was bearing fruit.

"Circus Ground, Super Cub Charlie Uniform Bravo is ready to taxi for a banner pick-up and a local flight to Niagara Falls."

"Charlie Uniform Bravo, Circus Ground, you're cleared to Runway 24, wind calm, altimeter 30.09, taxi Delta Bravo for an intersection departure off 24."

"Uniform Bravo."

I taxied out and completed a pre-take-off check. There was one other aircraft in the circuit.

"Circus Tower, Charlie Uniform Bravo is ready for takeoff, request a short circuit for a low and over the infield."

"Charlie Uniform Bravo is cleared for takeoff, wind light and variable, short circuit approved. Check the Piper Warrior on the crosswind ahead, call downwind for the low and over."

"Uniform Bravo."

I took off and flew inside the Warrior pilot's pattern. On my downwind leg I set up 75 mph and tossed the hook and cable out the door. Then I

The Super Cub jerked and accelerated into a climb.

held my headset with my left hand, skidded the airplane with my right foot and leaned out to check the cable. It was fine. I closed the door, did a pre-landing check and called the tower.

"Uniform Bravo downwind for a low and over south of Runway 24."

"Cleared for a low and over, Uniform Bravo, the wind is calm."

"Uniform Bravo."

I turned the Cub, descended and headed for the flags. I could see Chainsaw's truck parked to one side. The big kid was leaning against it. I leveled at 30 feet above the grass, wiggled in my seat and got ready to pitch up with full throttle.

Flying that low trailing a hook felt as comfortable as scud running through an antenna farm. I concentrated on skimming my tires over the centre of the rope with minimal correction. I nailed it perfectly. I applied full power and pulled back on the stick. During the pitch-up I reached down ready to yank the release lever.

I could feel the hook catch. I smiled to myself. The airplane slowed. I pushed the nose level and checked the airspeed indicator. It was below 70 mph and was dropping rapidly. Before I could pull the release, the Cub jerked and then accelerated into a climb. I could feel the blood draining from my face.

"Uniform Bravo, it looks like your rope separated at the tailwheel," the controller said. "The banner started to lift and then dropped back to the grass."

He must have been watching with his binoculars.

"Uniform Bravo, thank you," I replied. "Request a short circuit for a landing on 24."

"Short circuit approved, Uniform Bravo, you're number two behind a Warrior turning left base for a touch and go. Call downwind."

I landed and taxied to the ramp.

Our banner equipment included a box of short fabric loops made from the same material as the straps sewn into each letter. They were safety links. Ziggy had shown us how to attach them to the grappling hook cable and the release mechanism.

"This is the weakest part in the banner setup," Ziggy had said, "not counting the pilot. If you snag something and are not quick on the release, this is supposed to break. Never tow without one."

Chainsaw met me by the hangar in his pick-up truck. He stepped out holding the grappling hook and cable. There was a piece of ragged red strapping on the end of it.

"Looks like the safety link broke," he said.

I checked under the Cub's tail. The other half of the shredded link was attached to the release hook.

"So Charlie, what did we do wrong besides make a longer banner?"

The monster 14-year-old looked at his feet and scuffed the ground. "Well, sir," he answered shyly, "I wasn't here when you and Henry practised so I haven't seen what I'm suppose to see during a pickup."

"You're right."

"But would the calm wind make a difference?" he asked.

"Yes, it would."

"The grass is long, too."

"I hadn't thought of that."

"How about the temperature?"

"It's warmer, which doesn't help."

Chainsaw held up the parted safety link. "How often are we supposed to change these?"

"That's it, Charlie! Ziggy told us to change them every two or three tows and I forgot about it. I'll get another one from the hangar. You go and reset the banner."

"OK," he replied, handing me the cable and hook. He jumped into his truck and roared off.

I rigged a new safety link on the cable and attached it to the aircraft. The time was one-thirty.

Charlie had the banner reset by the time I was in the air.

"Uniform Bravo, downwind for a low and over south of 24."

"Uniform Bravo is cleared a low and over, remain south of Runway 24, there's a Cherokee on a wide base for a touch and go."

"Uniform Bravo."

I concentrated hard on my final approach. Ziggy had told us that too much speed might break the safety link during the pickup. My speed was right on, the altitude looked good and I flew my tires over the centre of the rig. The hook snagged the rope. I pulled up and reached for the release. The Cub jerked and then accelerated away without the banner.

"It looks like the same thing happened," the controller said.

He gave me a landing clearance when the Cherokee was clear of the runway. I met Chainsaw at the ramp. He held up the broken link.

We stood there silently for a moment, then Chainsaw said, "Didn't you say this equipment is used?"

"Yes, why?"

"How used are these links?"

"Charles, you are a genius! Even if these links haven't been used, they could be weak from age."

"Where do we keep them?"

"I'll show you."

We walked into the hangar. I pulled out the box of links from a cupboard in the corner. Chainsaw picked one out. He held its loops between his index finger on each hand and pulled. The fingers turned white and his face red. He grunted under the strain.

"Charlie, those have a minimum 500-pound pull resistance," I said. "You're not going to..."

"Snap!" went the strap.

"It wasn't hard to break," he said.

I thought for a moment. "Can you break two at once?"

He picked up two links, slipped them over his fingers and pulled. Nothing happened.

"Good," I said. "That's our answer. Toss those in the garbage. I'll take two fresh ones."

I rigged the double links to the release and the cable. I climbed into the Super Cub and looked at the clock. It was two p.m. I started the engine and called the ground controller for taxi instructions.

I tried to force myself not to hurry. It didn't work very well but I managed to hit the pick-up rope more or less at 75 mph and straight. Then I pitched up with full power. I felt a tug, reduced the nose up angle and watched the speed. It dropped to 70 as the Cub strained for a couple of moments, then it held steady.

"It looks like a clean pick-up, Uniform Bravo," the controller said. "Call clear of the control zone to the southeast."

"Uniform Bravo, thank you."

I looked ahead. I was still very low despite having the throttle shoved all the way forward. The trees, wires and buildings looked close. The airplane was barely climbing.

Ziggy had said that a twisted banner would slow us down. I dared a gentle turn to the left and slid open the window on that side. I stuck my head out and looked back. The banner was snaking, twisting and fluttering like a Congo line but it was readable. The altimeter indicated that I was less than 200 feet above the ground.

Chapter Twenty-one

Dancing with elephants

The Cub felt like it was climbing in quicksand. The best it would do was 50 feet per minute up and only if I held the controls steady. At that rate I would not reach 1,000 feet above ground before arriving over the Falls. I couldn't believe that a warmer temperature and seven extra letters could milk that much performance from the airplane.

I tugged back on the stick looking for more lift. The speed slowed to 65 mph, the rpm dropped slightly and the Cub stopped climbing. I lowered the nose to regain 70 mph and lost 100 feet doing it.

I retracted the one notch of flap thinking the reduced drag might help. The Cub started to sink. I reset half flap but not before losing another 100 feet.

I continued in the ignorant belief that I could circle to gain height before arriving over the buildings surrounding the Falls.

The rpms were up and the engine sounded fine but the airplane was struggling. I did a cockpit check. The oil temperature was high but still in its green arc. I watched it for a few moments. The needle didn't move.

I pulled on the carburetor heat to check for ice. The engine dropped 100 rpm and the airplane lost 50 feet. No ice, carb heat off.

A lack of performance wasn't my only problem. The fuel quantity tubes on the left and right wing roots indicated I was losing gas faster than the engine should be burning it. There were two scales marked beside each glass tube, one for level flight and the other for when the airplane was parked on its tailwheel. I had started with three-quarters fuel showing in both tanks on the ground, about 27 gallons. I was drawing from the left side.

The Super Cub was plowing along in an attitude about halfway between level flight and parked. If I was right, I had burned nine gallons from the left tank in 40 minutes, including the two failed pick-up attempts. That was 12 gallons per hour. The rev counter indicated 2300 rpm. Normal fuel consumption at that setting was nine gph but "normal" didn't include towing a 90-foot banner on the end of a 200-foot rope and using full throttle to do it. I checked under both wings for leaking fuel but I couldn't see any.

Time to turn back? I asked myself. Not yet. I could lean the fuel flow with the mixture control. That would reduce the fuel consumption and maybe yield a little more power. I checked the oil temperature. Blast, it had been sneaking up. I tapped the glass. The needle jumped another width. It was getting close to the red line. I left the mixture control at full rich since leaning it would have made the engine run hotter.

Twelve gallons per hour gave me two hours and 15 minutes of fuel from start-up. If I made it back on the ground in an hour, I'd have about 30 minutes of fuel remaining. Turn around now? That would be easy but it wouldn't solve anything. I smiled to myself. At least the rapidly disappearing fuel load would make it easier to climb, until I ran out of gas!

I looked ahead at the city of Niagara Falls. My altimeter was twitching to 900 feet above sea level. It wasn't high enough. The terrain rose toward Niagara Falls. The higher elevation was the reason there was a falls. It dropped from 600 feet above sea level. I would need to be above 1,600 feet before I arrived there to be at the minimum legal height. Ziggy and I had climbed to 2,300 feet when we towed the practice banner around the Falls.

I was clear of the Circus Airport Control Zone. It was time to call in but I didn't want to give away my low altitude.

"Circus Tower, Charlie Uniform Bravo is clear of your zone to the southeast climbing to one thousand six hundred feet for the Falls."

"Charlie Uniform Bravo, Circus Tower, we check you're clear of the zone." I detected a smile in the controller's voice. "We've been watching your progress through the binoculars. When do you start climbing?"

Wise guy. "I've been climbing all the time. You're looking at an optical illusion."

"Yours or mine?"

OK joker, you come and make this thing climb, I said to myself. "I'll call you returning."

"Roger. I'll talk to you sooner or later."

I started a gentle circle to the left. The Cub stopped climbing as soon as I banked the wings. Flying straight was the only way I could gain height.

This flight was turning into a nightmare but I had to admire the little airplane. It was struggling under the drag of the banner but was winning some progress. Its "I-can-do-it" attitude was infectious. I became more determined to complete this tow as a revenue hour.

I started a zigzag pattern, climbing a little between the turns. Ten minutes later, I was at one thousand four hundred. The clock read two-thirty. High enough. I headed directly for the Falls.

The airspace around the popular tourist spot was busy but uncontrolled. There were four helicopter operations offering sightseeing flights, two on each side of the Canadian and American border. They flew between 1,800 and 2,200 feet above sea level using their own variations of clockwise racetrack patterns. The larger companies often had two machines in the air at once and another one loading.

Airports on both sides of the border were bases for fixed-wing aircraft companies like The Flying Circus that also sold sightseeing rides over the Falls. They usually circled at 2,500 feet.

It was popular for airliners on the short-haul run between Buffalo, New York and Toronto, Ontario to fly by Niagara Falls at 3,000 feet as a treat for their passengers.

The United States Air Reserve launched their fighter aircraft toward the scenic pattern from their base five miles to the northeast. It wasn't unusual to see a pair of Voodoos on afterburners blast through the pattern.

To complete this mix, private airplanes transitioning the area would dive into the circuit at any time, from any direction and at any altitude. One thing was certain, everyone was looking down at the mass of water going over the cliff.

The helicopters were on different company frequencies, the fighter pilots listened to the military control tower, the airliners were talking to Buffalo Arrival and Departure and the rest of the airplanes could be on any frequency or none at all.

I had planned to fly at 2,300 feet, above the choppers and below everything else. I entered a clockwise pattern to circle around the downtown areas on either side of the Falls at 1,500 feet above sea level or 900 feet over the ground.

I selected the frequency for the largest Canadian helicopter company. Its pilots would be climbing and descending through my altitude.

"Traffic at Niagara Falls, this is a Piper Super Cub entering a clockwise pattern at the Whirlpool towing an advertising banner at one thousand six hundred feet." I fudged the altitude to make it sound less illegal.

I knew from piloting sightseeing flights in our Cessna that the helicopter pilots considered the frequency and the lower altitudes their exclusive domain. Two helicopter pilots made position reports in response to my transmission. I looked around and picked them out slightly above me, one coming and the other going. Then the company owner came on the frequency. I recognized his accent. We had met at the Circus Airport.

"Super Cub wid banner, dis is a private company frequency. Furdder more, you can't fly here at sixteen hundred feet."

"Hi Alfie. Please tell your guys to watch for a yellow and blue Cub trailing a message 300 feet behind. They can see me better than I can see them and they can manoeuver a whole lot easier."

"Banner airplane, climb to two tousand five hundred or leave da area now!"

The resolute spirit of the Super Cub got the better of me again.

"That's not nice, Alfie," I replied. "This airspace is public. You should learn to share."

"Who is dis?"

I had already said enough to stir up trouble. I continued to listen to the position reports but did not answer or call again. Alfie tried to raise me a couple more times and then gave up.

I headed upstream toward the Falls. It looked like I could reach down and touch the taller buildings. Mist from the base of the Falls rose above me. I stayed well to the left of the river and the waterfront.

I made my southbound turning point the Screamland Theme Park, a competitor to The Dome. I could see people walking between the carnival rides, exhibits, stage shows and food booths. I spotted two elephants being led around a small corral with kids on their backs. The animals walked like they were mechanical. I rolled out of the turn and flew downstream toward The Dome.

I had thought banner towing would be easy. There were no students trying to kill me and no sightseeing passengers with constant questions or unstoppable nausea. I was wrong. I was busier than ever.

On the straight stretches I concentrated on gaining altitude to make up for losing it in the turns. The engine was still at full throttle. The oil temperature was high but steady, helped occasionally by me flying in and out of the mist.

The fuel was another matter. The gas bobbed up and down in the indicator tubes. It was difficult to know the actual level, although it seemed to bob down more than up. At one hour into the flight and halfway through my towing hour, I estimated that I had less than 15 gallons remaining, about one hour. If I completed another 30 minutes of towing and flew back to the airport, dropped the banner, circled and landed, I might make it but I would be an idiot for trying. I decided that I would leave the Falls early and make it up to the customer somehow.

Each time I turned, I transferred my sunglasses to my shirt pocket, flipped up the window on the right side, stuck my head out and checked the banner. I was worried. The ribbon of letters seemed to be more active. It was gyrating and whip cracking. Maybe it was just the afternoon turbulence but it was getting worse. I watched for other air traffic during the

"This can't be good."

rest of my time in each circuit.

Summing it up, I was low on fuel, lower on altitude, high on engine temperature, towing a banner that was too long and too active. I had nowhere to go but down and nothing underneath but buildings, people and the world's most famous waterfall. Why was I here and what else could go wrong?

The answer to the second part of that question came silently but suddenly. I was turning over Screamland, looking down at the elephants plodding around their circle. The Cub suddenly zoomed forward like it had afterburners of its own. The feeling was the same as when the safety link broke during the failed pick-ups.

I continued the turn and looked behind in time to see the banner fluttering toward the ground. The weighted lead mast was pulling the letters from a horizontal banner into a vertical streamer.

"This can't be good," I said out loud. The whole rig weighed less than 50 pounds but it appeared to be accelerating. I circled and watched. The banner was going to land in Screamland with a message from a competitor. There would be hell to pay.

I could see that the letters were drifting toward the elephant ride. My spine tingled and my stomach flipped as I watched the lead mast plummet into the dirt in the middle of the elephant coral. The 100 feet of lightweight lettering fluttered into a pile around the mast.

I pictured two panicked elephants crashing through the wooden railings and charging across the midway grounds leaving a trail of trampled tourists. Screamland would have its own stampede. It would be the end of banner towing and the death of The Flying Circus.

I held my breath. The guys leading the elephants glanced at the pile of red letters while their animals continued walking at the same pace. I watched as the last piece of banner flopped across their path. The first elephant to reach it took a half step and then planted both front feet on the letters without spilling any of the kids off its back. Then it stood there. The other elephant stopped behind it. The handler tugged on the first elephant's lead rope. The animal didn't move.

I rolled the Cub out of its turn on a heading for home. I retracted the flaps and pushed the nose into a shallow dive. No worrying about oil temperature or fuel now. I had to get back to the airport as soon as possible.

I discovered that speeding up the Cub was like throwing feathers. The most I saw was 100 mph. I changed frequencies and called the tower.

"Circus Tower, Super Cub Charlie Uniform Bravo, returning from Niagara Falls for a landing."

"Charlie Uniform Bravo, Circus Tower, active runway is 24, wind calm, altimeter 30.10. I have a Warrior in the circuit and a Cessna 172 departing the zone to the southwest. Are you inbound for a banner drop?"

"Uniform Bravo, negative on the drop but please pass a message to the office that the banner is Code Red at the Screamland elephant ride."

"Ooookeyyy doookey," the controller said, dragging out his reply. "The message is being passed. Call joining the circuit for a landing."

"Uniform Bravo. Has Alpha November Delta returned from the cross-country."

"Affirmative."

"Thank you."

Henry and I had arranged for "Code Red" to be our signal that we had dropped a banner after Ziggy had warned us that we would. The return of Alpha November Delta meant that Henry had come back from his trip. Hopefully he was in the office or not too far away to get the message. I kept the Cub's speed up all the way to the circuit.

"Uniform Bravo, I check you're joining the downwind, you're number two to the Warrior on short final doing a touch and go."

"Uniform Bravo with the traffic."

I kept my approach in tight, landed on the main wheels, turned off the runway with the tail still in the air and taxied to the ramp. There was nobody around. I hotfooted it out of the Cub and into the office. Summer McDay was standing behind the counter.

"Henry and Charlie got the message," she said quickly. "They're on their way to Screamland."

"That's great."

"What happened?" she asked.

The phone rang. Summer picked it up. "The Flying Circus."

She listened for a moment. "Yes it is."

The caller started yelling. I couldn't make out words but the volume was unmistakable. Summer pulled the receiver away from her ear. Her face reddened as the caller ranted.

I thought it might be someone from Screamland. I signaled to the young college student that I would take the call. She waved me off with a shake of her head. She tried to answer the man. "I completely understand, Mr. Arsoneau."

He continued his tirade. Summer listened for a few more moments. Then the guy must have paused for breath; she jumped in.

"Does your daughter Amy know you talk to young ladies like this?"

Silence.

"I didn't think so. How about the police; do they know? They will when they hear your threats on this recorded phone call."

"Click."

Summer heaved a big sigh. "He hung up."

"Who was it?"

"That charming man was the manager of Screamland. Now I know where the name comes from."

"What did he say?"

"When I told him this was the banner company, he went berserk. He threatened financial ruin and physical harm to everyone here. Then he invited me to commit an impossible anatomical act with the banner which, by the way, he said we would never see again. Those weren't his exact words but you get the idea."

"Wow! I'm sorry you had to handle that. I could have talked to him."

"It wouldn't have made any difference. He was stuck on transmit."

I smiled at her moxie. "What's with this business about a recorded telephone?"

Summer grinned. "It's a girl trick to get rid of nuisance callers."

"Well, it worked on this guy. Who's Amy."

"Amy Arsoneau. She's in my course at school. I knew that her dad ran Screamland. Now I know why she cowers when someone shouts."

The telephone rang again.

"My turn?"

"Sure, go for it."

I picked up the receiver, "The Flying Circus."

It was Gus Drover from The Dome. The background was noisy on his end but his volume was louder.

"Hear that? It's a zoo in here!" he whooped. "Sign me up for an hour every weekend afternoon from now to the end of June. Then we'll talk about every day in the summer."

"I'm happy it's working for you, Gus."

"Not as happy as me! Gotta go." He hung up.

"At least the banner customer is satisfied," I said to Summer. "He wants the service every weekend."

"That's great!"

"It would be except we don't have enough letters to make up the same banner and I don't know why the last one broke lose."

"Can you order new ones?"

"Yes, but I don't know how soon we can get them."

"You'll know when you call the supplier. Maybe they can help with the breaking problem."

Henry and Chainsaw pulled into the parking lot in the Pinto. I couldn't believe that I was looking at a rolled up banner sticking out of the trunk.

"Banner rescue at your service," Henry announced as he stepped into the office.

"There must be a good story here," I said. "We were told to kiss that banner goodbye."

"By who?"

"The manager at Screamland," Summer replied. "At least that's what he told me on the phone, along with a few other things."

"We never saw any manager."

"How did you scoop the banner?" I asked.

"Charlie and I drove to the service entrance at the back of the theme park. We stopped by the maintenance building and a guy in coveralls came out. He asked if he could help us. I said that we'd come for the misguided advertising banner.

"'Follow me,' he replied.

"We did. He led us to the elephant corral. The banner was piled in the middle except for the tail end blocking the path. One of the elephants was standing on it. 'We can't get her off it,' the maintenance man said. Two handlers were trying to coax the animal to move with handfuls of hay, a bucket of grain and carrots. It wasn't working.

"'There's your banner,' our guy chuckled. 'You can have it if you can get Old Gloria to get off it.'

"Chainsaw asked me if he could try something. I didn't know what he had in mind but before I could answer, he stepped between the fence rails, walked up to the hay in front of the beast and picked some of it up."

"Where is Chainsaw now?" I asked.

"Putting the banner in the hangar. Anyway, the old elephant eyed him as he carried some hay to the railing and dropped it outside of the corral. He returned to the pile and gathered up some more. I swear that elephant glared at him. She leaned forward but didn't move her feet. Chainsaw dumped that hay and returned for more. The elephant stepped toward him. Chainsaw jumped through the rails. The old girl lifted her trunk and bellowed."

"Wow, he's lucky he didn't get hurt!" Summer exclaimed.

"Then the kid picked up some hay and offered it to her over the fence. She watched him for a minute and then took it. He led her away from the banner with more hay."

Chainsaw opened the door and entered the office.

"Hey, here comes the elephant tamer!" I cheered.

The youngster blushed and grinned.

"So where did you learn animal training, Charlie?" I asked.

"At home," he answered shyly.

"You raise elephants at home?"

"No," he laughed. "I help my mom with my younger brothers and sisters. She taught me not to reward bad behaviour. It works better when you take something away."

"Way to go Charlie!"

Chapter Twenty-two

Four solutions

"I have three problems," I said to Darcy Philips on the phone Monday morning.

"Let me guess. You wanted to fly. You didn't know how. You tried it anyway. Now you want me to fix something. What did you break this time?"

"Nothing. I towed a banner on the weekend. The Cub engine was down on power, high on oil temperature and high on fuel consumption."

"How many letters were you towing?"

"Thirty-two."

"What was the rpm with full throttle?"

"Two thousand, three hundred."

"I have four solutions."

"Shoot."

"One: never tow more than 30 characters. Two: take the Cub's prop to Happy Propeller in Toronto and get it re-pitched four inches finer. Three: we need to add a cooling lip under the engine cowling."

"How do you know all that?"

"That's the way it is: you're the pilot and I'm the mechanic. You create problems; I fix them."

I never could tell when the sarcastic mechanic was joking.

"You're kidding, right?"

"Not this time," he laughed. "Ziggy called me after flying with you guys. He told me your Cub would need a finer pitched prop and better cooling in the summer heat or when you tow too many letters. And here you are."

"So the finer pitch on the prop takes care of the low power problem, but what about the high fuel burn?"

The mechanic heaved a loud sigh. "What do you think the full throttle fuel consumption should be?"

"It was 12 gallons per hour!"

"Sounds right. Try towing a 100-foot banner with your Volkswagen. Then you'll learn about full power fuel burn."

"What's the fourth fix?"

"You lose weight but we both know that won't happen. We'll try the first three first."

"Joker."

"Hey, if I didn't laugh at you guys, I'd be in an institution. When can you get the propeller to Toronto?"

I looked at the booking sheets. Everyone was busy except me, on my day off.

"Thursday morning."

"I'll let them know you're coming. They can twist and balance it while you wait. Don't forget to take the Aircraft Technical Logbook."

"When can you do the cooling thing?"

"It's a simple fix. I'll make the piece today and install it the next time I'm down there. I can put the prop back on during the same visit."

"OK, but we'll need it soon. We have another banner tow booked this weekend."

"Thirty characters max?"

"I'll work on it."

Next, I telephoned Barney Swallow, the ancient aviator installed as our airport manager.

"Barney, when are you going to cut the grass south of Runway 24?"

"Never. Who's calling?"

"A paying tenant trying to make money towing banners from your infield."

"What's wrong with the grass?"

"It's too long. The letters snag on it."

"Do you rent the grass?"

"No."

"Shorten it yourself."

He hung up.

Henry telephoned the banner equipment company that same morning. He told me about it later.

"First: the shelf life of the safety links is several years but they are not dated so it's best to buy new ones.

"Second: it doesn't help to double them.

"Third: the banner gyrations are caused by faulty tails. The tailpieces are aerodynamic. They're designed to lift the banner to keep it horizontal and to hold it steady. The guy said whenever the tails are repaired some of the shape is lost and the banner goes wild. Then the safety links break prematurely."

"He got that right," I said.

"So I ordered a box of links, two new tails and several vowels to replace the ones that have patches on the patches."

"Thanks."

"The guy also said that a Super Cub towing 35, seven-foot characters would need a finer pitched prop and better cooling on a standard temperature day."

"It sounds like he knows what he's talking about."

Chapter Twenty-three

Super copter

Darcy assumed that Henry or I would unbolt the Cub's propeller, drive it to Toronto, wait for it to be re-pitched and drive home. Spending a day battling big city traffic in a temperamental old car didn't appeal to me. I decided to fly the Cub to Toronto Pearson International Airport on Thursday morning.

At the time, Canada's busiest airport allowed any aircraft to fly in and out. Most pilots of small airplanes were smart enough to avoid the area but I decided that I could go anywhere with the mighty Super Cub. Besides, Happy Propeller was handy to the general aviation area at the north end of the big airfield.

I departed at eight o'clock and followed the shoreline of Lake Ontario at 1,500 feet. A strong wind had kicked up from the southwest giving me a quartering headwind. The Cub's airspeed indicator read 90 mph with a 65 per cent power setting of 2350 rpm in level flight. I did a groundspeed check. It was 55 mph. I looked at the traffic on the highway below. I could have been down there passing me in my car.

I settled in for a long, bumpy flight. At least it was an opportunity to check the oil temperature and fuel consumption without the drag of a banner. So far, they were both normal. I spent the rest of that leg looking at the farmland waking up to spring and mentally kicking myself for not having telephoned a certain single schoolteacher in the last 10 days. I decided that it wasn't really my fault that I hadn't called Carol Thomas. I had worked long hours every day since meeting her. Now what could I say if I did phone her?

"Hi, we met at Melville Passmore's wedding. I'm phoning because I'd like to see you again but I'm really busy at the air service. Do you have time for me in September?"

I selected the Toronto International Airport information frequency before making the turn northeast bound at the end of Lake Ontario. The recorded Information Lima said that Runways 24 Left and Right and Runway 23 were active. The surface wind was 230 at 30 gusting to 35 knots.

I turned northeast and climbed the Cub to 2,500 feet, high enough to enter the Toronto Terminal Area at the outer ring. Then I switched to the VFR Terminal frequency.

"Toronto Terminal, Super Cub Sierra Charlie Uniform Bravo is by the Burlington Sky9way Bridge at 2,500 feet squawking 1200 inbound for Toronto International with Information Lima."

"Air Canada 139, turn to 265 for the intercept, you're cleared ILS 24 Left."

The controller was working two positions at once, IFR and VFR Arrivals. Replies from the airline pilots didn't come up on my frequency. The double duty controller continued talking.

"United Express 233, behind the Airbus, turn left to 290."

He worked two other aircraft before me.

"VFR Super Cub, descend to 2,000, turn left to 020, vectors for Runway 23, squawk 5512."

"Charlie Uniform Bravo."

I set up the turn and the descent and switched my transponder to 5512. I continued to hear the one-sided IFR transmissions. I let the airspeed build up to 100 mph in the descent hoping that I could impress the controller. His radar would show that the tailwind was giving me a 140-mph ground speed. If that didn't impress him, he might park me in a corner of his airspace and forget me. I leveled at 2,000 feet and set the power to 2450 rpm.

"Charlie Uniform Bravo is level 2,000."

"Charlie Uniform Bravo, radar contact. Expect to join the right downwind for 23."

"Uniform Bravo."

I was being vectored across and under the traffic departing Toronto's parallel runways. I could see the airport. Soon, I was told to switch to the tower controller for landing sequencing.

"Toronto Tower, Charlie Uniform Bravo is with you at 2,000."

The controller responded as if I was an airborne epidemic. "Charlie Uniform Bravo, confirm it's a Piper Super Cub?"

"Affirmative, Uniform Bravo."

"And you want to land at Pearson International?" His voice rose at the end of the question.

"Affirmative, Uniform Bravo."

"Turn left to 360 degrees, vectors for the right downwind to Runway

23, Uniform Bravo."

He was turning me away from the airport, parking me in a corner.

"Uniform Bravo."

So the controller didn't like handling slower traffic. He should have known that Super Cubs don't take up much airspace and can be landed on a dime. I started thinking like a righteous Cub pilot.

"Two can play this game," I said to the airplane.

I turned to the new heading, waited one minute and then countered its effect by slowing to 70 mph. The lower speed increased the drift in the strong wind giving me the same ground track as before.

The controller was busy on the same frequency handling all the traffic taking off and landing on three runways. I reached the right downwind, turned right and applied more power.

"Charlie Uniform Bravo is right downwind 23."

"Charlie Uniform Bravo?" Mr. Big-Airplanes-Only sounded surprised. "Downwind already? Did you miss the left turn I gave you?"

"Negative, Uniform Bravo."

"Better slow down, Uniform Bravo. It will be a while before I can fit you in."

I think I was supposed to say, "Forget it," and go somewhere else. "Uniform Bravo," I replied. I considered being told to slow down as a victory for little airplanes.

"You're currently number five, Uniform Bravo, behind a Learjet presently 14 miles back for 23."

Maybe it wasn't a victory. He was doing a good job of keeping me discouraged.

"Uniform Bravo."

"Air Canada 139, cleared to land, Runway 24 left."

"Cleared to land on the left side, 139."

The battle wasn't over yet. I reduced the power, raised the nose and extended full flap. I trimmed the Cub to hang from its propeller at 45 mph. Then I turned the airplane 180 degrees and flew into the wind.

On a heading of 230, the Cub floated slowly backward over the ground. The controller's radar would show that I was tracking 050 degrees at five mph. This went unnoticed for several minutes before someone in the tower must have picked up the binoculars.

"Charlie Uniform Bravo," the controller barked, "what are you doing now?"

"Uniform Bravo is flying downwind, slowly," I said.

There was a long pause. "Charlie Uniform Bravo, you're number four following the Learjet."

"Negative contact, Uniform Bravo."

Of course I couldn't see the traffic. It was still ten miles away and I was flying with my back to it.

"United Express 233, cleared to land 24 Right."

"Cleared to land 24 Right, 233."

"Charlie Uniform Bravo, what airspeed can you give me on final?"

"Anywhere from 30 to 85 knots, Uniform Bravo."

That translated from a minus five to a plus 50-knot forward ground speed. The other traffic would be approaching at 100 to 120 knots over the ground.

"This is not going to work, Charlie Uniform Bravo."

This comment made me want to be as uncooperative as the controller.

"Then I guess a ramp landing is out of the question," I replied sarcastically. I figured that I'd be kicked out of the control zone next.

An older, calmer voice with an American accent took over the position. He must have been a supervisor. He cleared an aircraft to position on 24 Right and then cleared the airliner ahead of the Learjet to land on 23. That made me number two if I was still on the list.

"Charlie Uniform Bravo, Toronto Tower," the older voice said, "would you accept an arrival on Juliet Taxiway at Kilo? You will have 2,000 feet of Juliet running parallel to Runway 23."

It was 1,990 feet more than I needed in this wind. I looked down. I was already opposite that intersection and it was close to my destination on the ramp. I replied quickly and with as much confidence as I could muster, "Affirmative, Uniform Bravo."

"Fine, Uniform Bravo, maintain your position for now. You are number two to land following the Learjet on final to Runway 23. Do not cross Runway 23."

"Hover north of 23 without crossing," I read back, "Uniform Bravo."

I increased the power and retracted one notch of flap. The Cub stopped drifting backward and hung over the ground. I ducked my head down and looked rearward under the wing. I could see the landing light on the Learjet. It was the first time I had been sequenced to land after traffic that was two miles behind me.

The supervisor continued working other traffic. "Bearskin 99, check you're by the marker, you're number four for Runway 23 behind the 747, break; Air Canada 124, to position and wait Runway 24 Left."

"To position 24 Left, 124."

"United Express 233, turn right at the first available highspeed and call one point niner."

"Two three three."

"Charlie Uniform Bravo, maintain your position and start your descent, number two to the Lear."

"In sight, Uniform Bravo."

"Learjet Bravo Alpha India, cleared to land Runway 23, plan to exit at

Papa or further. There will be an aircraft landing behind you on Juliet. The wind is 230 at 30."

"Alpha India."

"Lufthansa 550 continue, you are number two for 23 behind the Learjet touching down."

"Fife fife zero, roger."

"Air Canada 124, cleared for takeoff 24 Left, wind 230, 30 gusting to 35."

"Cleared to go, 124."

"Charlie Uniform Bravo, land at your discretion on Juliet holding short of Papa. The wind is 230 at 30, peak gusts to 38."

"Uniform Bravo."

I cut the power and pushed the nose down to maintain a near zero forward speed. The turbulence was stronger close to the ground. I worked the Cub's stick like I was churning butter. The airplane responded to every input but it also obeyed every gust.

"Charlie Uniform Bravo, there is a 747 on a two-mile final for 23."

I ignored the controller and concentrated on riding the Cub down to the taxiway.

"Bravo Alpha India, I check you're clearing at Papa, thank you, call ground point niner."

"Alpha India."

"Lufthansa 550, you will see an aircraft arriving ahead and to your right on Juliet Taxiway. You are cleared to land Runway 23, wind 225 at 35."

"Lufthansa fife fife zero."

I added power to slow my descent. I touched down on Juliet past the Kilo turn-off. I pulled the throttle back and retracted the flaps to stay down but I had to continue flying on the ground as gusts rocked the Cub.

I managed a quick radio call. "Charlie Uniform Bravo on Juliet."

"Charlie Uniform Bravo, thank you, call ground twenty-one niner."

"Uniform Bravo."

My right hand and both feet were dancing on the controls. I fought to hold the airplane in place while changing radio frequencies.

"Charlie Uniform Bravo is with you on Juliet going to the government ramp."

"Uniform Bravo, roger, taxi at your discretion along Juliet and Kilo."

"Uniform Bravo."

"Learjet, Bravo Alpha India, you are now cleared Juliet and Kilo to the ramp. Follow the Super Cub. He will be turning onto Kilo Taxiway also."

"Alpha India."

The next challenge was taxiing down Juliet to Kilo. I reduced the power further and released the brakes. The airplane began to roll back-

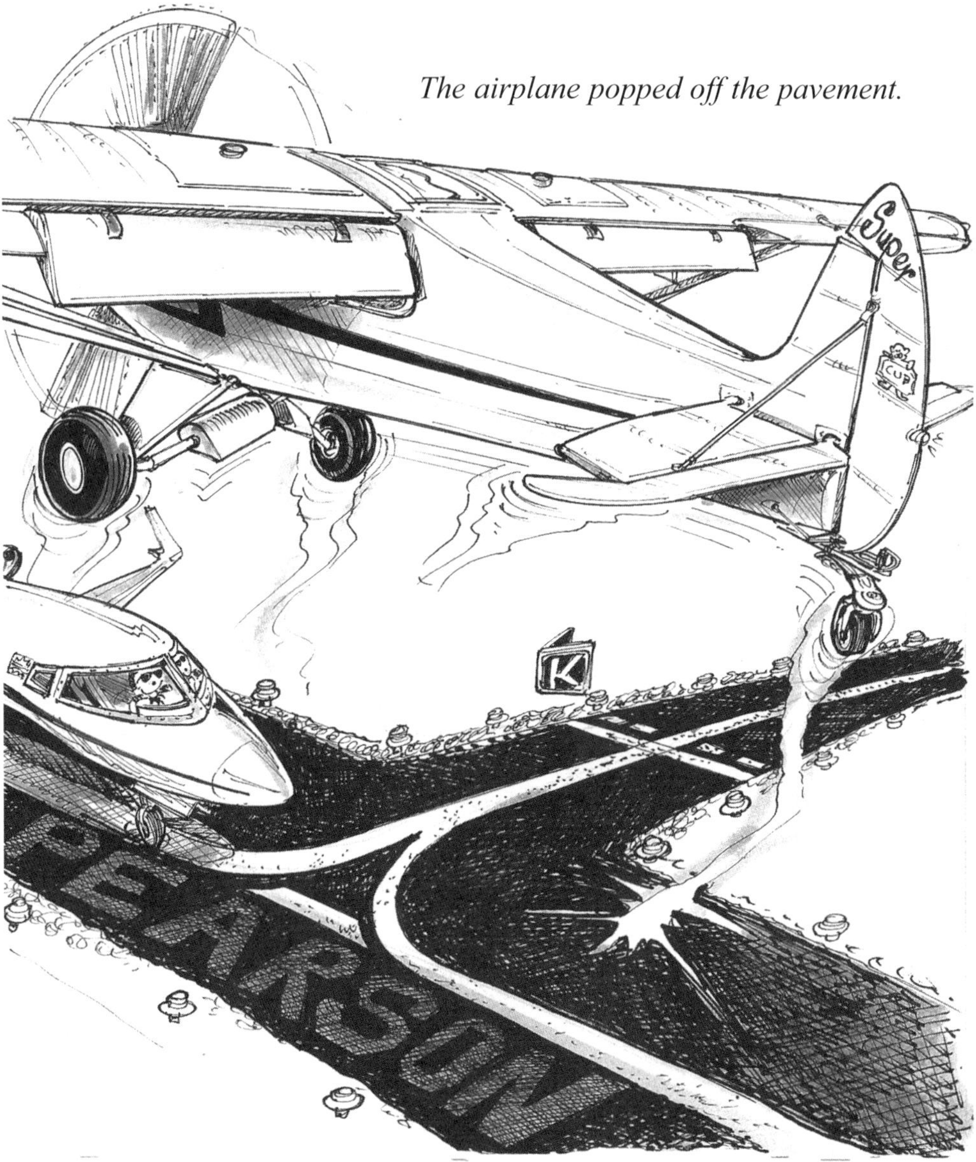

The airplane popped off the pavement.

ward. It gave a little wiggle as the castering tailwheel swung around. I steered with reverse commands to the rudder. To correct to the right, I applied left rudder, the wind pushed the tail to the right and the main wheels rolled backward in that direction. I continued to work the control stick when gusts tried to lift the Cub off the ground. The result was a snake dance but the zigzagging allowed me to look behind to see where I was going.

In the meantime, the Learjet had started a fast taxi down Juliet. The two airplanes were going in the same direction but were facing nose to nose with a narrowing gap. The Learjet drew close enough that I could see the two pilots staring at me from their cockpit. They did not look pleased. I was holding them up with my wayward taxiing.

I knew it would be impossible to turn the Cub away from the wind to travel up Kilo. How did I get myself into this situation? I asked myself. I could think of only one way around it. At the intersection, I added power and extended full flaps. The airplane popped off the pavement. The Learjet pilot's eyes widened as they watched me rise in front of them.

I banked slightly to the right and crabbed sideways along Kilo. Taxiing backwards was hard enough. Flying sideways along the taxiway and making it look like I was on the ground was nearly impossible. The Cub and I were rocking and rolling, dipping and diving, jumping and jiving. It must have looked like I was flying a mechanical bull.

"Charlie Uniform Bravo, are you on the ground or in the air?" the ground controller asked.

"Affirmative," I replied.

"Are you OK to taxi in this wind?"

"Affirmative."

At the first ramp, I pulled ahead and landed.

"Toronto ground, Uniform Bravo is holding off Kilo for the Learjet."

"Thank you Uniform Bravo, break, break; Alpha India, the Super Cub is holding for you."

The Lear pilots blasted by my tail without acknowledging.

"Uniform Bravo is cleared to the ramp behind the Lear."

"Uniform Bravo.'

I let the Cub roll backward and then continued my sideways flight along the taxiway to the government ramp. I landed, retracted the flaps and taxied forward to a tie-down spot sheltered from the wind by the hanger.

I shut down the engine and sat holding the controls. The Cub continued rocking gently but was no longer rolling. I jumped out, grabbed some ropes from the baggage compartment and tied the wings and tail to the cables on the ground. So far so good.

Chapter Twenty-four

The twist

Removing and reinstalling a fixed-pitch propeller is not difficult. I had done it before. It required a screwdriver, wire cutters, torque wrench, lock wire and a little knowledge on how to use them. Do it wrong and all that rotating energy could rip the propeller off the airplane. So the job required a maintenance engineer's signature to be legal. I planned to get one, after flying to Derry.

I had parked at the Department of Transport ramp. It was a risky place for a bit of amateur maintenance but it was closest to Happy Propeller, the least used on the busy airport and the only ramp with free daytime parking. I counted on it to be mostly deserted mid-morning. It was. The government inspectors based there had flown to other airports or departed on local flight tests.

I zipped off the nose cone with an electric screwdriver, cut the lock wire and ratcheted out the bolts. The propeller pulled off the hub when I rocked it with my hands. I laid it on the ground, stashed my tools in the Cub and grabbed the Aircraft Technical Logbook. Then I hoisted the prop onto my shoulder, walked through the gate and headed up the street.

An old station wagon with faded fake woodgrain on the sides slowed going past me half a block later. It pulled over and stopped. The driver's door opened and a slim, older man dressed in clean work clothes stepped out.

"Headed for Happy Propeller, are you?" he asked. His tone was friendly.

"Yes, sir," I replied cautiously.

The man walked to the back of the wagon and dropped the tailgate. "I'm going there too," he said. "Slide her in and I'll give you a ride."

I stopped in my tracks and frowned at this stranger.

"Oh, I should introduce myself. I'm Hap Track," he said, "from Happy Propeller. You must be The Flying Circus guy that Darcy Philips called about. I recognized your Super Cub prop."

I shook the man's outstretched hand with some relief, unshouldered the propeller and slid it into the wagon.

"Hop in," Hap said.

"Thank you."

Hap Track turned out to be a friendly man in a quiet way.

I hoisted the prop onto my shoulder and headed up the street.

"How did you know I was going to your shop?" I asked for fun.

"Lucky guess," he smiled.

"Do you always cruise the airport roads looking for business?"

He smiled again. "After this morning, maybe I should."

Two blocks later, Hap parked beside a modern industrial building. He opened the back of the wagon, I retrieved the propeller and followed him into a small, clean shop. Five other men were busy at different propeller workstations. Most looked up and nodded our way. Hap nodded back.

My host walked over to an unused metal table. "Place it here," he said. He donned a shop coat from a nearby hook and went right to work.

I watched for the next hour while Hap measured, filed, twisted, re-measured and balanced the Cub's propeller. He worked silently and methodically, giving me the impression that he was performing a time-honoured ritual rather than a job. He finished by stamping and signing an entry in the propeller section of the Technical Logbook.

"Follow me," he said.

We walked to a front office where I was introduced to a middle-aged bookkeeper.

"This is Buela Babcock," he said. "She will invoice Darcy Philip's shop and ask you to sign it. I'll give you a ride to the airport when you're done."

"Thank you, sir."

I found out that it was Miss Babcock, executive assistant to Mr. Track, president and owner of Happy Propeller. I signed the bill and walked back into the shop.

Hap was listening to one of the workers. He looked my way.

"All set?"

"Yes, sir."

We drove the three blocks to the airport in silence. Hap pulled through the gate at the government hangar. I didn't really want him to see that I had flown the Cub rather than carrying the prop in another airplane.

"This is fine right here," I said. "Thank you for the great service." I reached for the door handle.

He stopped the car. "You're welcome. Would you like some help re-installing the propeller?" His voice and expression stayed neutral.

I blushed. "No, I've done it before."

"OK."

We both climbed out of the wagon. Hap opened the tailgate. I pulled out the prop.

"Have a good flight."

"Yes, thank you again."

He smiled. "You're welcome."

It took me half an hour to install the prop and lock-wire the bolts. The time was twelve o'clock.

I was lining up the screw holes to mount the nose cone when a government car appeared from around the corner. A Department of Transport logo was painted on the door.

The car slowed going past the front of the Cub, turned and parked on the other side of the airplane. Inspector Kennedy climbed out of the driver's seat. He was wearing his usual rumpled, dark suit and frown. He walked toward me.

I felt like I was standing there without any clothes on. I stopped what I was doing and silently hoped that the difficult man remembered being nice during his base inspection the previous week.

"Regulations prohibit non-certified personnel performing unsupervised maintenance on aircraft," he declared bluntly.

Technically there was nothing illegal with what I was doing until the airplane flew but I had no intention of arguing the fine points of aviation law with this professional enforcer.

"Good afternoon, sir," I replied.

"Show me the documents for this aircraft," he said sharply, holding out his hand.

"The same ones that you inspected last week?" I asked with restrained sarcasm.

"That is correct."

I walked around the wing strut, reached into the cockpit and retrieved the Aircraft Journey Logbook from the baggage compartment.

"The documents are in the pouch at the back," I said, handing him the book.

Kennedy removed the documents and tucked them under his arm. He opened the book to the current page, turned the book around and held it up for me to see.

"There is no entry showing that the airplane flew here from Circus," he snapped.

"That's correct," I replied.

I legally had 24 hours to mark in my flight.

His frown deepened. He leaned forward and looked inside the Cub.

"Is that the Technical Logbook for this aircraft on the back seat?" he asked.

"Yes, sir."

"Regulations prohibit carrying the aircraft's Technical Logbook in flight," he declared.

The sour man had no immediate proof that the airplane had been flying that day.

"Yes, sir," I replied.

"Show it to me."

I reached into the airplane and handed him the book. He opened it to the Propeller Log and scanned it. His enforcer's scowl melted into puzzlement. He snapped the book closed and handed it to me along with the Journey Log and documents.

"Humpf!" was all he said.

With that, he walked around the corner of the hangar and out of sight.

"Good day, sir,' I replied.

I hurriedly flipped open the Technical Logbook to see what had deflected him off his warpath. The Propeller Log contained an entry for the pitch change, overhaul and balance of the propeller. The removal and reinstallation of the prop were also included. Hap Track had covered my lawless ramp work with his own qualified signature.

Chapter Twenty-five

Performance, good and bad

I taxied the Cub for takeoff without going airborne. Toronto Ground Control cleared me down Kilo to hold short of Juliet. The wind had dropped a bit but it took full right stick and full opposite rudder to prevent weather cocking. I used a series of power bursts and braking to wiggle the Cub to the intersection.

"Switch to tower now, Charlie Uniform Bravo."

"Uniform Bravo."

I changed frequencies. The same friendly American voice was already calling me.

"Super Cub Charlie Uniform Bravo, will you accept a departure on Juliet from Kilo? You have 2,000 feet remaining, the wind is 250, 25 to 30."

"Affirmative, Uniform Bravo."

"Charlie Uniform Bravo, depart Juliet from Kilo at your discretion. Straight out departure, do not cross the departure path for 23, advise level at 1,500."

"Uniform Bravo."

Ready or not, I wasn't going to miss the chance to make two firsts in one day: a taxiway landing at Canada's busiest airport and now a takeoff. I extended full flaps. I didn't need them but I wanted to show off by making the Cub's short take-off ability shorter. I hit full power. The airplane leaped off the asphalt. My heels were still holding the brakes. I eased the nose down to pick up speed. The engine roared. The rpm nudged the red line at 2700. I pulled the nose up. The Cub rocketed skyward. I reached 1,500 feet in less than a minute and throttled back. It was then I realized that the finer pitch on the prop was giving higher rpm and kick-butt climb performance.

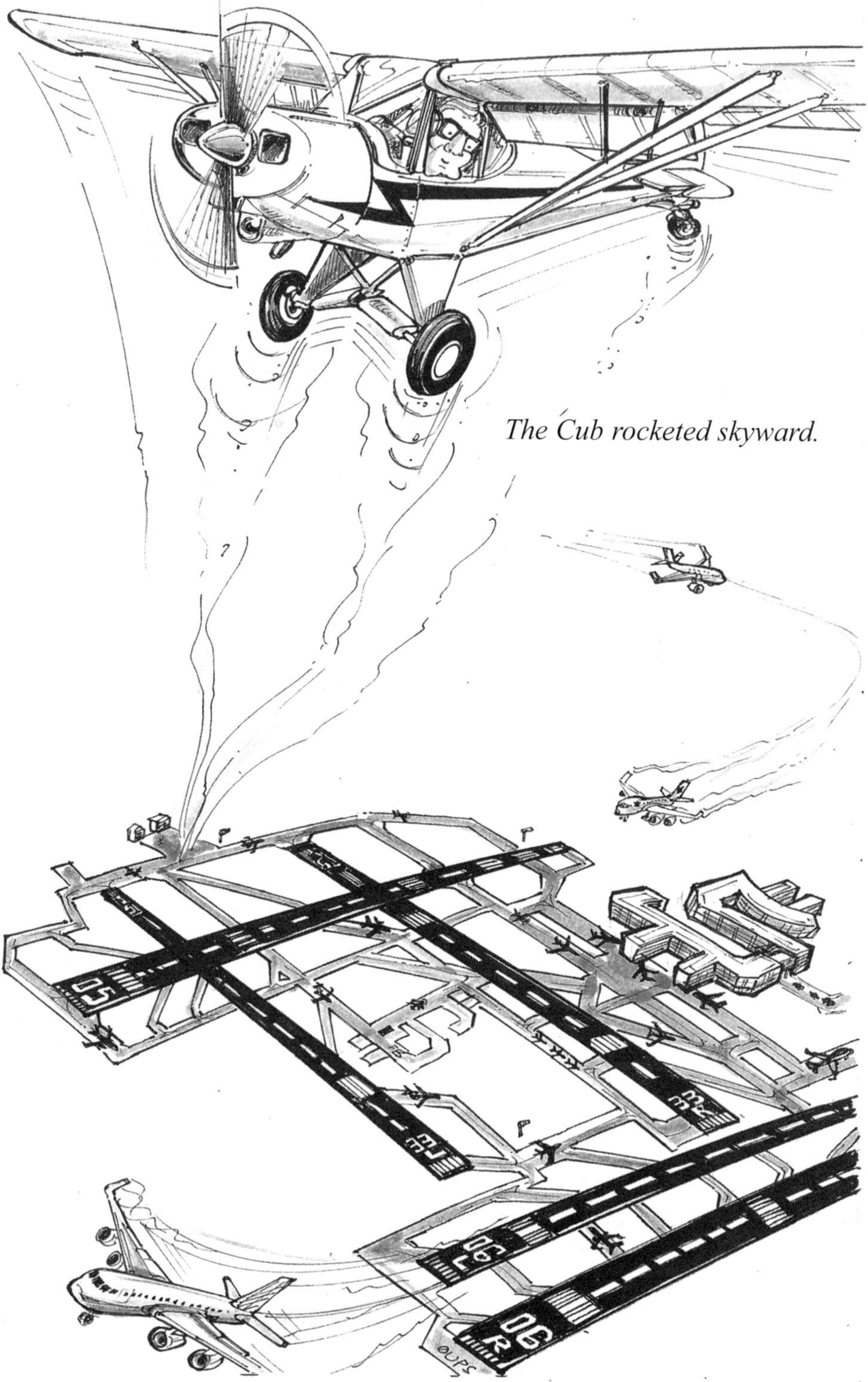

The Cub rocketed skyward.

"Uniform Bravo is level at 1,500."

"Charlie Uniform Bravo, roger, left turn to 220 degrees, you are cleared across Runway 23, maintain 1,500 feet."

"Two two zero, cleared across 23, maintain 1,500, Uniform Bravo."

I was heading for the Derry Airport. There I hoped to have Darcy's cooling lip installed.

The Cub was slower in cruise, much slower. A power setting of 2350 rpm produced only 70 mph in level flight. Wow, I thought a 20-mph cruise penalty was a lot to pay for added climb performance. I looked around the cockpit. The flap handle was in the extended position. I swore as if someone else had forgotten it.

I released the flaps. The speed increased and so did the rpm. I reset the power back to 2350. The speed settled at 85 mph, which was much better. I was cruising slower than a speeding bullet but five mph was a fair price to have an airplane able to leap tall buildings in a single bound.

The ground speed was another story. I stayed low to duck some of the headwind but it still took most of an hour to fly a no-wind, 30-minute trip.

I shut down the Cub in front of the open Derry Air hangar. Darcy Philips walked out to meet me.

"Hey, if it isn't Hector the Airplane Wrecker," the joking mechanic said. "I thought you were taking this prop to Toronto for a pitch twist."

"I did," I said, climbing out of the front seat.

"Sure, and I'm going to Alaska for lunch."

"No, really. I flew the Cub there, had the prop done and flew here. I thought you might add the cooling lip so we'd be ready for towing banners this weekend."

Darcy looked at the propeller on the airplane. He noted the smooth, shiny leading edge. He rolled his eyes. "Now I suppose you want me to sign off your installation work."

"Not this time."

I told him the story of flying to Toronto, removing the prop and meeting Hap Track and Inspector Kennedy.

"You should be in jail," he declared, shaking his head.

"I think it was close."

"I'll get the cooling lip."

I looked under the Super Cub's engine cowling where Darcy's modification would be attached. There was a space between the lower cowling and the firewall where the engine cooling air exited. The added lip was to draw more air out.

Darcy strutted back two minutes later carrying a curved piece of sheet metal about ten inches long in his hand. He reached under the cowling for a couple of seconds and then stood up.

"All set," he grinned.

"That's it?"

"Yup, let me show you."

We both bent down.

"It's a piece of sheet aluminum," he said pointing to the curved metal, "held by two spring clips riveted to one side."

"That won't stay put in flight."

The smiling mechanic slid the lip off and handed it to me.

"Let's see you open one of the clips, Hercules."

I couldn't. Darcy took it back and reinstalled the lip in the cowling opening.

"You can adjust the amount of lip extended into the slipstream until the oil temperature stays well below the red line. Slick, eh?"

"Slicker than snot on a doorknob," I replied.

Darcy laughed and slapped me on the shoulder. "I'll see you tomorrow. I'm going to Circus to help Rock rig his floats."

The flight home was quick. I used the Cub's improved climb power to zoom up to 5,500 feet where the tailwind was stronger. The oil temperature gauge read a needle-width lower. About halfway home, I eased the nose down and traded the altitude for more airspeed. I was on the ground by one thirty.

A yellow bus was pulling into our parking lot as I taxied in. Leanne must have scheduled a school class trip.

The kids were regular springtime visitors at The Flying Circus. Teachers were happy to escape their classrooms in the warmer weather. They loved to book airport field trips. Leanne had been a public school teacher before her children were born. She always obliged the teachers when they called. She also sent handouts for the appropriate grade level to the school before the visit. From these, the kids and teachers understood that the tours were interactive. They came expecting to learn.

Leanne conducted the tours herself but any flying instructor caught on the ground was fair game. "Oh look, there's a pilot; let's ask him questions," she would say.

I understood the importance of involving the community in aviation but I didn't feel obligated to participate on my day off. I parked the Cub at the fuel pumps beside the hangar. I was hoping to fill it and escape toward home before meeting up with the group.

I took too long. It was impossible to hurry our small refueling nozzle. I finished and headed for the office. I rounded the corner of the hangar and came face-to-face with a class-size mix of chattering eight-year-olds, five adults and Leanne.

My scan of the group stopped at one of the adults walking behind the students. She looked like Carol Thomas. Our eyes locked. She was Carol Thomas. Seeing her was a total surprise. Carol blushed and showed a tiny smile. I was embarrassed and pleased at the same time. I was happy to see Melville Passmore's favourite schoolteacher but felt immediate guilt for not having called her since we had meet.

"Let the man through girls and boys," Leanne said. "Next we'll see where the airplanes are refueled."

She was sparing me a question period on my day off.

Carol watched the kids and then our eyes locked again. She appeared a little uncomfortable with the encounter. Leanne led the group on. Carol walked over to me. She spoke first. The words tumbled out quickly.

"I tried to call you here last week. I wanted to take my class on an aviation field trip. I checked with our nearest airport but they don't allow class tours so I spoke to Melville Passmore who told me that your flying school did."

She took a breath. Her face was flushed and the wind was blowing her hair back. She looked beautiful in a natural sort of way.

"I phoned for you but Mrs. Rains said you were flying. She asked if she could help so I mentioned the class trip and she booked us right away for today and sent some wonderful background material for the visit."

Carol seemed nervous. Her unease was letting me forget my guilt. I started to smile.

"I would have talked to you first but it seemed like a good opportunity for the children and you had mentioned that you usually took Thursdays off so I didn't expect to see you here."

The smile spread across my face. I liked not being the awkward one this time.

"I hope you don't mind me bringing the class," she continued. "I didn't want you to think I was taking advantage of having met you to book this tour but Mrs. Rains was so accommodating..." She stopped her run-on explanation. "Why are you smiling?"

My mouth went to full grin. "I've never seen you ill at ease."

She frowned. "Well, I didn't want to appear too forward."

I was going to tell her not to worry but that's not what came out.

"You look good," I said. I took a chance and touched her right shoulder. "I'm glad you called for a class tour and I'm happy that I was here."

Carol blushed a little more. I think I did too.

"So you don't mind?"

"No, I don't. I enjoyed meeting you at Melville's wedding... and I... I should have called you before now."

This was followed by an awkward silence.

"About what?" she asked.

Oh, boy. Could I ever get comfortable with this straight shooting country girl? I wanted to.

"Ahhh... I thought we might get together again?"

"Oh... sure... yes... that would be nice." The frown lines were melting away. "Well, I'd better get back to my class."

I didn't want her to go. I was enjoying meeting her on my home turf.

"Leanne will take good care of them," I said hopefully. "Come into the office for a minute. I'll record my flight times and we can talk."

She hesitated and then let out a deep breath. She looked up at me and said, "Would you mind talking to the kids for a few minutes instead? I know they'd love to hear from a pilot."

Meeting her class wasn't the first thing on my mind. "Ah... no... not at all," I replied.

I followed her to the fueling area. The students were gathered around the Super Cub. Leanne was asking them questions about the airplane as it rocked gently in the wind. They were distracted by the re-appearance of their teacher.

Carol nodded at Leanne and then spoke to the children. "Class, this is one of the flying instructors." She introduced me. "Does anyone have a question for a pilot?"

A half-dozen hands shot up.

Carol pointed to one. "Yes, Christine?"

The princess of a girl looked at me and asked, "Are there girl pilots?"

"Yes, of course," I answered. I tried to deepen my voice to sound more like a pilot. "Ladies can fly airplanes as well as men."

The pretty little student frowned. "Where are they?" she asked.

"Ah... there... there are girl flyers everywhere," I stammered. The class looked around. "But not here right now."

Carol came to my rescue. "Good question Christine. We will make it a class project to learn how girls and boys become pilots.

"Yes, Peter. You have a question?"

The kid looked older than the others.

"My dad said flying is dangerous," he announced.

I didn't know that kids' questions could be so tough, I thought to myself. I tried stalling. "What is your question, Peter?" I asked.

"Is he right?"

"Peter," Carol said, "we've talked about there being danger in everything. Danger is why we look both ways for traffic before we cross a street. Pilots look for danger when they fly to keep their passengers safe."

Carol was back in her element. I was spiraling out of mine.

She asked another girl for her question. "Amanda?"

"How much money do you make, Mr. Pilot?"

Carol glanced at me.

I was determined to show her that I could handle questions from eight-year-olds. I blurted out the first thing that came to my mind. "Well, Amanda, right now I'm not making any money. This is my day off and I just finished a non-revenue maintenance flight."

That was it for the kids. They stopped paying attention and started talking, kicking at stones and bumping each other.

Carol held her hand straight over her head and stared at them. The moving and talking stopped. She nodded toward Leanne. "We will finish our tour with Mrs. Rains so we can stay on schedule," she said. She looked at me. "Thank you... ah... Mr. Pilot."

"You're welcome."

"OK, girls and boys," Leanne announced, "next we will visit the weather office. Everyone in single file, please. Follow me."

Carol gave me a quick, motherly smile and joined the end of the line. I returned a weak grin and headed for our office.

Summer McDay was manning the flight desk and sewing patches on damaged banner letters. Her greeting indicated that she had also been watching out a window.

"I see you met Mrs. Thomas," she said in a sing-song voice.

"Yes, I have," I replied, "and the monsters in her class."

"They seemed well behaved to me," she offered.

"Here are my flight times on the Cub and the fuel numbers." I dropped the gas pump clipboard on the desk.

"Yes, sir, I'll get right on it." It was a mockingly serious reply.

I was pushing the Cub into the hangar when the class returned from the weather office. I walked over as the kids were filing into the bus.

Carol smiled at me. "I'm sorry the kids' questions didn't work out too well," she said.

I pretended that it was no big deal.

"The questions were fine but I'll have to work on my answers."

She laughed and then covered her mouth in case she shouldn't have.

I changed the subject. "How do you manage your motion sickness on the bus?"

"Oh, it's no trouble," she replied.

"It's a long ride from here," I suggested hopefully. "I'm headed home. I could drive you if you'd like."

"Well, thank you but I'll be fine. I found the answer to school bus motion long ago." She saw that everyone was on board. "Bye for now," she said. With that, she climbed the steps, glanced at the kids, sat down in the driver's seat, started the bus and drove off.

Chapter Twenty-six

Pick me up

My Volkswagen Beetle died on my way to work the next morning. First the engine misfired, "Bumpf." A few seconds later it went, "Bumpf, bumpf."

I was approaching Courier Hill so I pushed on the gas pedal. The engine surged and burped again. "Bumpf, bumpf, bah bumpf."

"Come on baby, you can do it!"

"Bumpf bah dah bumpf, vrroomm, bumpf."

Our forward speed decayed as the Beetle started up the hill. I floored the accelerator. The engine revved but gravity was gaining the upper hand.

"Bumpf bah dah bumpf, vrroomm, pop, bumpf, pop, bumpf." The little car bucked and slowed. Then the engine caught again.

"Come on," I coaxed, "you have to make it."

I didn't have time for this. I was on my way to the Circus Airport to teach a full day of flying lessons. My first student was booked at eight-thirty and it was eight o'clock already.

"Vrroomm, bumpf, bah dah pop, bumpf... pop, gasp... vrroomm."

Each time the car bucked, the rusted fenders clapped in unison. I downshifted into third gear.

"Vrroomm, pop, vrroomm, bumpf, pop."

I downshifted again. The engine sputtered and the fenders flapped but we were nearing the top of the hill. I rocked in my seat. "Come on baby!"

"Pop, bah dah pop, vrroomm, pop, gasp... vrroomm, pop, pop."

"If we don't make this last little bit," I yelled at the car, "I'm going to step out and let you roll backward into oblivion!"

"Vrroomm, pop, vrroomm."

We crested the top. I eased my foot off the accelerator. The engine died immediately. I depressed the clutch pedal and coasted down the other side. We picked up speed. I tried combinations of gears and throttle, letting the clutch out each time. The engine fired but would not run.

Courier Hill was a one-stoplight town. The intersection was partway down the hill. The light was red. I braked to slow down, willing the light to change.

It did but too soon. I let the car roll. It accelerated like a tree falling, slowly at first. I leaned forward.

I could see there was another car stopped at the cross street. My light turned yellow when I was still several car lengths back. The other car stayed put. I rolled on. The light turned red as I hit the intersection. I continued through and down the hill.

There was an old fashioned, two-bay service station at the bottom. I braked, turned in and coasted to a stop.

Both garage doors were open showing one car up and another down. A medium-sized, middle-aged man in greasy dark blue coveralls and a welder's cloth cap stepped out from under the car on the hoist. He stopped at the open door and wiped his hands slowly with a dirty rag. I climbed

"Come on baby, you can do it!"

out and walked toward him. He squinted into the morning sun.

"Hi there," I called to him.

"Howdy," he answered cheerfully. "What kin I do fer ya?"

"My car died coming over the hill," I explained, waving my thumb back at the VW. "Could you have a look at it?"

"I'm lookin' at 'er now," he grinned and chuckled, "but she's still ain't runnin', hee, hee, hee."

I returned his smile and pretended to enjoy his small-town humour.

"Leave it with me," he said. He tilted his head toward the cars behind him. "I'll get a look at 'er b'fore long."

"May I use your phone?"

"Local call?"

"To the Circus Airport."

"Should be OK." he nodded at the rounded office next to the bays. "Help yerself."

Henry was scheduled to open our office that morning. I checked my watch. He would be pulling out the airplanes now. I picked up the grease-covered receiver and dialed the number. It rang several times before he answered.

"The Flying Circus," he puffed.

"Hi Henry, it's me. My car quit at Courier Hill. Any chance you can come and pick me up?"

There was a pause. "Ah, sure," he replied slowly. "Where are you exactly?"

"At the old service station near the bottom of the hill going toward Circus."

"I know the one," he replied. "I'll leave a note for your student and be there soon."

"Thanks, I owe you."

I stepped into the garage. "I got a ride," I called out to the mechanic. I held out my business card. "Will you phone me when you find out what the Bug needs?"

He walked over. "Yes sirree, Bob!" He grinned and stuffed the card into the top pocket of his coveralls.

"Thank you."

He nodded and ducked back under the car.

I went outside. It was a beautiful spring morning. A bright sun was warming the chilly air. I sat on a bench in front of the little office and soaked up some rays. I thought about how lucky I was to have Henry as a friend and business partner. We were both working hard. If we could get the banner towing business off the ground, we might see some black ink on the books.

I checked my watch again. Fifteen minutes had passed since I had called the flying school. Henry should be here in another 15 to 20 minutes, I thought to myself. I closed my eyes.

A few minutes later, a shadow flicked across the sun. My eyes popped open. There was movement just above the horizon. I squinted. A low flying airplane was banked in a descent over the strip plaza on the edge of town. It was the new Super Cub, unmistakable with its yellow and blue mix of colours.

The wings leveled as the little airplane lined up parallel with the road. It was in a silent glide toward an open field across from the service station. I stood up as it got closer. It was the Cub for sure and Henry was flying it.

"The crazy bugger," I whistled under my breath.

I ran toward the plane. As a pilot from populated Southern Ontario, I didn't think about landing on anything but airports. There had to be something illegal about what I was witnessing but this wasn't the time to ask. I sprinted across the road and hopped the ditch.

I got there just as Henry pulled up to the roadside. The split door on the right side was open. My partner swung the airplane around. I ducked under the flap and dove into the back seat. He kept the engine running.

"Good morning," Henry called out.

"Go, go, go!" I shouted to him as I dug for the seat belts. "Let's get out of here!"

"OK, hang on!" he yelled and added power.

The Cub shot forward. Its large tires bounced a few times over the lumpy ground and then it hopped into the air. Henry banked the airplane toward Circus. I struggled to fasten my belts while being pummeled by the chilly wind through the open door. Henry held the control stick between his knees, reached out with both hands and pulled the door closed.

"That was pretty slick," I said.

"The Flying Circus at your service," he laughed.

Henry radioed the control tower as we approached the five-mile zone around the Circus Airport.

"The runway is your choice, Charlie Uniform Bravo. I have no other traffic, wind calm, altimeter 30.09." The controller was Barry McDay.

"I'll take Runway 06," Henry replied.

"Cleared for a right base to Runway 06, Uniform Bravo. Call on final."

My partner flew a tight circuit, was cleared to land and touched down near the exit to our ramp.

"Cleared in," Barry said. There was no mention of where the Cub had been or what Henry had done.

"So, are we in trouble?" I asked Henry as we were climbing out of the airplane.

"For what?"

"Oh, how about low flying over a built-up area," I said, "for starters."

"Flying low is a legal part of landing and taking off," he replied calmly. "Back home I would have landed on the road and pulled into the service station."

"So why didn't you?"

Henry grinned. "Some city slicker might think it's illegal."

"It is."

"There you go."

My first student was sipping on a cup of coffee when we walked into the office.

"Good morning," I said. "Thanks for waiting."

"No problem."

The telephone rang. I answered it. "The Flying Circus."

It was the auto mechanic from Courier Hill Motors. He sounded very excited.

"The-cops-just-left," he stammered, jamming the words together in a squeaky high voice. "They're-lookin'-fer-a-downed-plane. I-don't-wanna-know-if-yer-in-trouble, but-I-thought-I-should-tell ya. I-said-we-seen-nothin'. Did-I-do-right?" He took a breath.

I replied to what I thought he said. "Yes, absolutely. You did the right thing." I tried to sound calm and honest. I assured him that nobody was in trouble. Then I thanked him for his loyalty to a customer that he had just met.

I hung up. The phone rang immediately. I picked it up.

"The Flying Circus."

"Barry here. The sheriff is on the other line. He's asking about a yellow and blue plane going down near Courier Hill. Is there anything that you'd like to tell me about your flight?"

"Oh, you want to talk to Henry," I replied. "Hang on."

I held out the phone. "It's Barry. The sheriff is asking him about an airplane going down near Courier Hill."

Henry smiled and took the phone. He related the conversation to me later.

"I told Barry that your car had broken down in Courier Hill and I had picked you up in the Super Cub."

"Is he going to log a violation?" I asked.

"There's nothing to log. Barry's a farm boy; he understood but he appreciated knowing that he could tell the sheriff no one had crashed."

"OK, thanks for taking care of it."

"You're welcome." Then in mock seriousness he said, "You'd think these city people had never seen an airplane land before."

"Well, I'd bet it's the first time an airplane landed in that field."

Henry chuckled. "We could change that. Let me know when your car's ready to be picked up."

There were no more phone calls about a downed plane. It appeared that we had gotten away with it.

Later that morning, the mechanic from Courier Hill Motors called back. "Yer car's fixed," he announced in a more normal voice. "It was just the ignition condensor. She's ready to go."

"OK, thank you," I replied. "Please leave the key in the ashtray. I'm not sure when I'll be able to pick it up."

"Are ya comin' by plane?" he asked hopefully.

"It depends on what we can work out here."

"Kin ya let me know? I'd sure like to see it agin."

"I'll try."

Henry and I squeezed time from the schedule to go for the car that afternoon.

"The field is big enough to land and take off without backtracking," my partner said. "We can do a quick in and out."

"What's the rush?" I teased. "Back home you would have landed on the road."

"Back home nobody would have called the cops," he replied.

He went outside to ready the Cub. I phoned the service station and told the mechanic that we were flying in for my car.

"Hot diggity!" he shouted. "We'll be watchin' fer ya."

"Would you mind putting the key in the ignition?" I asked. "We want to make it quick."

"Yes sirree Bob!"

Henry was already in the airplane when I left the office. He started the engine as I climbed into the back seat. He radioed Circus Ground Control and asked for taxi instructions for a flight to Courier Hill.

There had been a shift change. The controller must have been new to Circus Tower.

"Runway 06 for Super Cub Sierra Charlie Uniform Bravo, the wind 090 degrees at five to ten, altimeter 29.86, taxi Delta Charlie Bravo for an intersection departure. Say again the destination."

"Courier Hill, ten miles south of here," Henry replied.

The controller didn't answer right away. Henry started taxiing.

"Ah, we don't have an airport listed for Courier Hill, Charlie Uniform Bravo. Do you know the identifier?"

"Affirmative. It's Charlie Hotel Mike, but it won't be on your list," he announced. "It stands for Courier Hill Motors. We'll be landing beside

Highway 20 outside of the village to pick up a car."

I could tell that Henry was amusing himself. His grin was wide enough that I could see it from the back seat.

"So this Motors place has an unlisted private airport?"

"Affirmative," Henry replied. "It's very convenient."

"Roger. Call the tower when you are ready for takeoff, Charlie Uniform Bravo."

Henry switched frequencies. "Charlie Uniform Bravo is ready to go, request Runway 24."

It was the same controller. "Ah, the wind is from 090 at five to ten knots, Charlie Uniform Bravo. Would you like Runway 06?"

"Negative," Henry replied, "Runway 24 is closer to where I'm going."

The controller paused. "Ahh, backtrack on Runway 24 is approved, Charlie Uniform Bravo. Advise ready to go."

"I don't need a backtrack," Henry answered calmly. "I'm ready now."

"From the intersection, you'll have 2,200 feet remaining on Runway 24, Charlie Uniform Bravo, with the wind from the east at 10 knots."

"Thank you. I'm ready to go," Henry repeated.

There was another pause. "Charlie Uniform Bravo is cleared for takeoff on Runway 24 from the intersection of Bravo with 2,200 feet remaining and the wind 090 degrees at eight knots.

Henry added power and taxied onto the runway. He turned in his seat toward me and asked, "How much do you want to bet the controller is not watching us right now?"

"Oh, he's watching all right."

Henry smiled and then let the Cub trickle down the runway an extra 100 feet before applying full power.

"Now you're teasing the poor guy," I called out.

Henry nodded.

The controller must have been unfamiliar with Super Cubs. The airplane had the same 150-horsepower engine as our Cherokee 140 trainers. Both airplanes had been built by Piper but the Cub carrying Henry, me and half fuel, weighed 1,500 pounds. The all-metal Cherokee with the same load would weigh over a ton and its wings were five feet shorter.

The Cub's take-off distance was 200 feet in no wind compared to 1,000 feet in a Cherokee. The 10-knot tailwind would triple each airplane's take-off distance. This was no trouble for the Cub but would have put a Cherokee off the end of the runway before it could get airborne.

We were off in less than 1,000 feet. Henry turned toward Courier Hill. Ten minutes later we were in a descending slipping left turn over the plaza. The Cub dropped like a brick. I had the door open and my feet out.

Henry leveled the wings just above the ground and pulled the nose up. The Cub plopped onto the field in a three-point landing. We jiggled to a

I hit the ground running.

stop close to the roadside. I hopped out and sprinted toward the garage. Henry applied full power. The Cub was airborne in a bounce and a skip.

I jumped the ditch onto the road and ran to the waiting Volkswagen. Movement at the service station made me look up. There were at least 20 people standing out front. They were waving at me. Some cheered. I could make out two dark coveralls and a uniform in the middle of the crowd. The sheriff's cruiser was parked nearby. The mechanic must have invited half the village to see the plane. I could feel my face flush with embarrassment. I waved in reply and jumped into the VW. The engine started on the first try. I beeped the horn at the crowd and sped off.

My eyes were glued to the rear view mirror. There were no cars following me. It looked like I had made a clean get-a-way.

What I didn't know, but would soon find out, was that two plainclothes federal police officers were staked out in the donut shop down the road. They had a clear view of the landing field and the garage. They had witnessed the whole thing.

Aviation regulations are a federal jurisdiction. Apparently the district supervisor did not check with the local police when he received a report of possible illicit airplane activity. He dispatched two officers to stake out the area in case the airplane returned.

Return we did. Our drop-off and my get-a-way were so quick that the federal agents were convinced we were up to something unlawful. They tripped over each other rushing out of the donut shop as I sped by in the Volkswagen.

If they had been familiar with my car, they would not have hurried. At 50 mph the old girl was working hard. I was watching for police so I saw the plain, dark blue Plymouth squirt onto the road well behind me. It caught up quickly but I didn't think much of it.

We were on a two-lane highway. The guy in the Plymouth was obviously in a hurry and wanted to pass but on-coming traffic prevented it. I accelerated out of courtesy. This did little to satisfy the guy as he pressed close to my bumper so I went faster. Sixty mph was flat out for the tired Beetle. Its fenders flapped in time to the vibration from the lumpy tires.

After a long curve, the Plymouth pulled out to pass. I looked over when it was along side. There were two guys in the front seat. The one on my side held a badge up to his window with one hand and was motioning for me to pull over with the other.

I didn't need any more convincing. I slowed and eased onto the shoulder of the road. The Plymouth stopped ahead of me.

Two dark suits opened their doors and approached my car cautiously on either side. I rolled down my window and placed my hands high on the steering wheel.

"Was that you who hopped out of the plane back there?" the skinny guy on my side asked.

"Yes, sir."

"Ahh... isn't that against the law?"

"No, sir," I replied. I hoped he didn't hear the unconvincing waver in my voice.

"My partner and I thought it was awful slick how that airplane dropped in and out of there so quickly. We figured you had to be up to something we should know about."

"Oh no, sir!"

His rounder partner looked in the car from the other side and then checked under the loose fenders.

"Step out of your vehicle, sir," my interrogator said firmly.

"I'd better get going"

I climbed out slowly.

"Turn around please," he said, "and place your hands on the car."

He patted me down like the cops do on television. His partner positioned himself in front of my car.

"Turn around," the officer said. "May I see your driver's licence?"

I eased my wallet out of my back pocket and found my licence. I handed it to him. He looked at it and then held it out to the other officer.

"So, tell me, just what were you doing?"

The squeaky voice that answered didn't sound like mine. I hastened to explain that I taught flying at the airport, that my car had broken down on my way to work and how an airplane pick-up seemed like a good idea.

"Flying can be very convenient," I offered. He frowned. "There is nothing illegal about landing an airplane off an airport," I added quickly, "but I'm sorry if we caused any trouble, sir."

"What is the name of the other pilot?"

I told him. He wrote it in his notebook. In the meantime, the heavy-set dark suit had ducked into the Plymouth. I presumed he was checking my licence. He stepped out of the car and nodded to his partner. It must have been a good nod.

"You are free to go," the first guy said, "but I'd like your phone numbers at home and at work in case there is a follow up."

I gave them to him. His partner handed me my licence.

I could hear an airplane coming from behind the two officers. I looked up. In the distance, the Super Cub was flying low to the horizon. It was descending toward us over the field across the road. Henry must have come back to check on me.

"Maybe it would be a good idea," the officer continued, "if you and your pilot friend stuck to airports rather than holding surprise aircraft demonstrations around the neighbourhood."

"Yes, sir," I replied quickly.

As I spoke, the Cub leveled off about 40 feet above the ground. It was headed right for us. Henry had the power on.

"Yes sir, you're absolutely right," I said. I opened my car door and hurried to get in. "I'll be sure to tell him."

With that, the Cub roared over our heads. The feds did not hear it until the last second. They did some serious ducking.

"#%*&@!" one of them swore over the receding noise.

"He's just seeing if my car broke down again," I shouted. "I'd better get going so he knows I'm OK."

I started the engine, engaged first gear and pulled onto the road. I watched my mirrors all the way to the airport.

Chapter Twenty-seven

Slick

Darcy Philips arrived on Friday in his pick-up truck. Rock Headley was riding with him. They were towing Rock's floats on a trailer. The unlikely pair worked in our hangar all morning. They hung Rock's Citabria a few feet off the ground, removed the landing gear and fitted two pontoons.

I was in the office when Darcy came in.

"What's the number for the control tower?" he asked Leanne.

She dialed it and handed him the phone.

"Hello, I'm calling from The Flying Circus. We're going to tow a floatplane on a trailer along Runway 24 for a departure."

"No, we're not? What do you mean?"

"Yes, I can spell 'N-O'. Can you say, 'Y-E-S'?"

I was having trouble believing what I was hearing.

"You think I need an airshow permit and a VHF radio in the truck? Well, there's a radio in the truck, how about one out of two?"

"No?" He reached over the counter and hung up the phone.

"Those guys are long on rules and short on usefulness."

"You want to tow the Citabria to flying speed on the trailer so Rock can lift off?" I asked.

"I did, but the tower won't let me," the mechanic replied.

"It sounds risky."

"It would have been the safest and quickest takeoff that the Citabria will see for the rest of the summer," Darcy said. "Rock plans to fly overloaded from his fishing camp all season with that small engine."

He looked at Leanne. "Can I have the control tower again?"

Leanne redialed the number and handed him the receiver.

"Hi, it's me at The Flying Circus again. I'd like clearance to tow that Citabria on the trailer to the infield for a grass takeoff."

"I can't call you from the truck, it doesn't have a radio."

Darcy smirked. "Oh yeah, I did say that, didn't I. Well, it's an AM/FM radio but the pilot can call you from the airplane. I'll watch for your lights crossing the taxiway."

"Thanks."

"So now you're going to pull the trailer to flying speed across the infield?"

Darcy let out a sigh. "No, but if you're so interested, come and help us."

We went outside.

The wiry mechanic explained to Rock that he couldn't take off from the runway. "I'll tow you over to the grass and you can try it from there," he said. "You ride in the Citabria and call for a taxi clearance. I'll watch for a green light."

"Sure enough," Rock said. He was grinning with anticipation. He hopped onto the trailer, then up to the right float and into the cockpit.

"You," Darcy said, pointing at me and then the truck, "come with me."

I got into the Fargo. Darcy jumped into the driver's side and started the engine.

I didn't know what was cooking but I was concerned. "Rock doesn't have a seaplane endorsement, you know," I said.

Darcy looked at me with a crooked smile. "Does he need one to take off on the grass?"

"I don't know."

"Would he know how to fly floats from grass if he did have one?"

"No."

"There you go. He's as qualified as you are."

He let out the clutch and headed for the taxiway. A flashing green light appeared in the control tower cab.

Darcy pulled the trailer to our banner setup area on the grass parallel to Runway 24. He stopped with the truck pointed into the light wind. We got out. Rock climbed down from the airplane.

Darcy unlatched the trailer from the ball hitch but left the chains attached. Then he fetched two lengths of rope from the back of the truck and handed one each to Rock and me.

"You guys tie these to the aft cleats on the floats. Then hold on and stand clear of the trailer."

I don't think Rock had any more idea about Darcy's plan than me but he was grinning as if he did.

"If you get off, where will you land?" I asked the muscled pilot.

The truck jerked forward and the trailer tipped

"At the camp," he answered happily. "I've got customers for this weekend."

Darcy started the truck. Rock and I stood behind each float hanging on to the rope. The mechanic popped the clutch. The truck jerked forward, the front of the trailer tipped up, the floatplane slid back and the chains pulled the trailer out from underneath it. Darcy turned the truck to the left and parked it. The unloading job was slick except for the rope marks on my hands. Rock didn't seem to notice his.

Darcy walked to the front of the floats carrying two large plastic jugs. He handed one to me.

"What's this?"

"Engine oil," he said. "Pour it in front of the right float. Rock, you climb in and get her warmed up."

Darcy took the cap off the jug in his hand and started pouring the black contents on to the grass leading away from the nose of the left float. "Use lots," he said to me. "There's more in the truck."

Rock started the Citabria's engine.

Six jugs later we had oiled a 100-foot path leading away from the floats. It didn't seem right to dump used engine oil on the grass. I expected Barney Swallow, the airport manager, to come charging out with a loaded shotgun.

"Wouldn't water do the same job?" I asked Darcy.

"Maybe," he chuckled, "but Rock doesn't have a seaplane endorsement."

Behind us, the happy pilot was doing a low-power run-up check. We walked back to the airplane. Darcy signaled him to move the stick back and forth. The Citabria rocked gently on its floats. The resourceful mechanic sloshed oil under the nose of the pontoons as they lifted and then moved to where Rock could see him. He held his arm straight up. Rock talked to the control tower, acknowledged their transmission, looked our way and nodded. Darcy squatted and dropped his arm forward like a launch controller signaling a catapult shot on an aircraft carrier.

The Citabria engine roared and the airplane shook but didn't move. Rock pushed the stick forward, the floats tipped onto the oil and the slide began. The airplane accelerated slowly at first. The rudder wiggled as Rock danced on the pedals trying to stay on the oil. Then the airplane picked up speed quickly, bumping along the rough grass. It lifted off and stayed in the air. Rock turned northward.

"That worked pretty well," I commented to Darcy.

The mechanic grinned. "Slicker than snot on a doorknob."

Chapter Twenty-eight

Chainsaw of fire

I noticed smoke rising from the Circus Airport as I was driving in Saturday morning. I floored the accelerator. The Bug rounded the corner onto the entrance road with tires squealing. There was a grass fire in the infield. It looked like the fire department had just arrived. Firemen were unrolling hoses from a pumper truck and a tanker stopped in the grass ahead of an advancing, jagged line of small flames. The fire was burning slowly over our banner pick-up area. Chainsaw Charlie was leaning on a shovel off to one side.

I parked my car at the edge of the ramp and hotfooted toward Chainsaw. The firemen were busily connecting hoses and running them from the pumper toward the flames.

Suddenly, twin fingers of flame and smoke shot ahead of the main fire in the direction of the trucks. The fire must have reached the two rows of oil that Darcy and I had laid down the day before. Half of the firemen decided to move the trucks and the other half continued setting up to fight the fire. The result would have made a good movie. Firefighters working the hoses were jerked from their feet as first one truck and then the other pulled away, in opposite directions. Hoses connecting the two separated. Fountains of water under pressure sprayed from their ragged ends. Grass snagged underneath both trucks was burning. It ignited more grass as the units retreated.

I stopped beside Chainsaw. He looked worried.

"Did you call the fire department?" he asked.

"No, I didn't. Did you light the fire?"

"Yes, I did."

I could picture what had happened. Chainsaw was from New

"You can be jailed and made to pay all costs."

Brunswick. The fire was his way of naturally trimming the growing grass. The youngster had lit the burn so it would travel away from the airport buildings, over the banner launch area and to a drainage ditch mid-field, which it was doing nicely, with help from the fire department.

The truck drivers stopped dragging the fire and the hoses around. They jumped out and foamed the flames underneath the vehicles with portable extinguishers. Meanwhile, the three firefighters who had been abandoned, hopped through the main flame front to the burned side. They trudged toward Chainsaw and me across the sooty grass in their full gear.

I put my hand on Chainsaw's shoulder. "It looks like your grass burning turned into a practice for the Three Stooges and friends."

The big kid turned to see if I was kidding.

"Look at it this way, Charlie; no one has been hurt and this scene is too funny to worry about," I said. "Here they come. We'd better wait and laugh about it later."

Chainsaw grimaced and said, "No, sir... I mean, yes, sir."

The shortest, roundest of the three fireman reached us first. He planted his boots well apart. The two others stopped behind him.

"Are you responsible for this fire?" the first man shouted with great authority.

"Yes, sir, I am," I replied.

I thought of thanking his men for spreading it, but I didn't.

He rummaged through the flaps and pockets of his coat and came up with a pencil and pad.

"What's your name?" he demanded gruffly.

I told him. He printed it on his pad.

"Do you know arson is a criminal offence?" he continued loudly.

Several smart-mouth replies about the proficiency of his crew popped into my head but I didn't have time to go to jail. I forced myself to think how Henry might handle this guy.

"Yes, sir," I replied, as seriously as I could muster.

Mr. Authority squinted at me menacingly. "You can be jailed and made to pay all costs associated with extinguishing this fire!"

"Yes, sir."

I could see that the two blackened fire trucks were now being driven clear of the flames. Chainsaw stood passively beside me. He was managing to suppress the churning that must have been going on inside. My lecturer continued.

"Did it occur to you that we're wasting valuable time and resources on this nuisance fire?" Now the fireman was barking like a drill sergeant. "This could be preventing us from responding to a real emergency!"

"No, sir."

He moved his smudged face closer to mine. "What'd you say?"

I said, "No, sir; it did not occur to me."

The trucks were parked on the ramp now. Firemen were checking the undercarriages for flames and shutting down the flow of water to the remnants of hose. The two men standing behind my lecturer started walking toward them.

My dressing down wasn't over.

"Obviously you were too dumb to notify the fire department of your intentions and to apply for a burning permit!"

"You are absolutely right, sir. I was."

"You bet your boots I'm right!" he roared. His rising blood pressure was turning his cheeks red under the smudges. "And furthermore, my men could have been injured for nothing fighting this fire!"

Behind him the grass continued to burn. The main flame front was merging with the fire trails left by the trucks.

"Yes, sir," I said. "That would have been unfortunate."

"Unfortunate?" he bellowed. "The blood of my men would be on your hands for the rest of your life!"

The firemen were unhooking and gathering up their shredded hoses.

"Yes, sir. I hope no one was hurt."

"If anyone was, you're going to be in bigger trouble than you already are!"

"Yes, sir. It was foolish of me to jeopardize your brigade with a grass fire."

Parts of the flame front were now reaching the ditch and fizzling out.

"And furthermore," he ranted, "this is an airport! Do you know how many calls we received from people thinking an airplane had crashed?"

"No, sir, I don't."

"Plenty! You'll also be charged with public mischief. You'll pay for wasting the department's time and the taxpayers' money!"

"Yes, sir."

The rest of the fire was burning itself out in the ditch.

"And a hefty fine on top of that!"

"Yes, sir, and may I say that your men did a fine job." I nodded toward the infield.

The round man turned. The flames were gone, the equipment had been stowed away in the trucks and the men were shedding their heavy coats. A few wisps of smoke rose from the edge of the ditch.

"We're lucky to have such a good crew near the airport," I added as sincerely as possible.

"You're darn right!" the man declared with less anger.

I motioned to the men and trucks. "I'm glad to see this excellent response in the event something really bad was to happen."

"We always do our best!" my lecturer declared proudly.

"I can see that," I said, extending my hand. "If there's anything I can do for the Circus Fire Department, I'd be honoured to help."

He held the gruff look on his face but accepted my handshake.

"Well, thank you," he replied.

"No, thank you!" I said, pumping his hand enthusiastically. "It's a pleasure to see the department on the job."

"I hope you've learned something today," he replied.

"Absolutely!" I declared. "You'll never have trouble from us again, I promise." I let go of his hand.

He smiled. "I'm glad to hear that." He stuffed his pencil and pad into a pocket with great purpose and then wagged a dirty finger at me. "Remember, no more grass fires."

"Yes, sir... I mean, no, sir! No more grass fires!"

He nodded his approval and headed toward the trucks.

Henry would have been impressed, I thought to myself. I turned and looked at Chainsaw. His face was locked into a serious expression.

"I think we dodged a big one there, Charlie," I said. "Don't let this upset you. The fire was a good idea. It's just that the airport was the wrong place for it."

He dropped his gaze to the ground, paused for a moment and then lifted his head. "The burn wasn't my idea," he replied quietly. "Mr. Rains told me to do it."

Chapter Twenty-nine

The trampled look

The equipment from the banner supply company arrived on Friday. We were good to tow on the weekend with new tails, fresh break-away links and some new letters.

The manager of the Niagara Falls Dome and I worked his advertisement down to 28 characters: "ELEPHANT STAMPEDE AT NF DOME". I was eager to tow the shorter banner with the changes to the propeller and cooling.

Chainsaw Charlie had come to the airport early on Saturday to burn off the grass before rigging the banner for me to tow in the afternoon. He started setting up as soon as the firemen left. I flew with students for the rest of the morning. Henry and Leanne were taking the day off.

I fastened a new break-a-way link to the Cub's tail. Chainsaw laid out the advertisement on the shortened grass in the airport infield. I was ready to fly the pickup by one o'clock.

I took off, tossed the hook and cable out the door, flew a tight circuit and lined up with the poles. I skimmed over the loop, opened the throttle and pulled back on the stick. The hook caught the rope and the Cub slowed. I lowered the nose with my right hand and held the banner release lever with my left. The link held and the Super Cub climbed away, slowly but steadily.

"It looks like a clean pickup," Barry McDay said from the control tower. "Call when you are clear of the control zone to the southeast."

"Uniform Bravo," I replied.

I slid open the left side window, held on to my headset and looked back. The new white tail on the banner was holding everything vertical and rock steady.

The finer-pitched propeller and shorter banner had increased the performance just enough. The Cub climbed slowly, including in gentle turns. I reached 2,300 feet by the time I was flying the racetrack pattern around Niagara Falls. This put me above the helicopters and below the other traffic. I throttled the engine back a touch from full power without losing altitude. The oil temperature stayed in the green and the fuel in the sight gauges did not plunge toward zero. If the link held I would have no worries. I was careful to fly around Screamland just in case.

My thoughts wandered to a certain modest but country-wise schoolteacher. I wanted to call her. I wondered how I could impress her instead of making a fool of myself.

Barry McDay's voice broke into my thoughts. "Charlie Uniform Bravo, Circus Tower, are you on this frequency?"

I fumbled for the transmit button on the control stick and swung the headset microphone against my mouth.

"Affirmative, Uniform Bravo."

"Summer called from your office. She requests that you return to base with the banner."

I could feel blood drain from my head. Now what?

"Do you know why, Barrie?"

"Apparently there is a problem with the letters."

I turned the Cub and stuck my head out the window. The banner was following me and riding perfectly. I couldn't read it from the aircraft so I couldn't check the lettering. I had no idea what might be wrong.

"Summer is on the phone," Barry added. "She says the request comes from the customer."

"OK, thank you. I'll call approaching the control zone."

There was nothing to do but speculate and fly back to the airport. I couldn't hurry in the Cub if I wanted to. I looked back at the banner a couple of times without seeing a problem.

Barry trained his binoculars on the message as I flew on the left downwind leg at 500 feet. "I'm reading it backwards but I wrote the letters down to check the spelling," he said. "It looks fine from here."

"Thanks," I replied.

"Charlie Uniform Bravo is cleared for a low and over south of Runway 24 for the banner drop, wind 230 at 10."

"Uniform Bravo."

I throttled back and began a gradual descending left turn down to 50 feet. I flew over the burned-out grass and pulled the release. The Cub shot forward.

"It looks like a clean drop," Barry advised. "Charlie Uniform Bravo is cleared for a short circuit Runway 24. You are number two following Cessna traffic on final for a touch and go."

I landed and taxied to the ramp. Chainsaw was waiting for me.

"I'll talk to Summer first," I said to him after shutting down.

Our part-time receptionist began talking as soon as I cleared the door.

"The Dome manager said that the banner was unreadable. He didn't want to waste money on it. I told him that I'd try to contact you to return."

"Did he say why it was unreadable?"

"All he said was that it looked like it had been trampled by elephants."

"OK, thanks. I'll go to the infield with Charlie and check it."

We saw the problem as soon as we reached the haphazard pile of letters. Charlie had placed them face down for the pickup. The letters were smudged from the blackened grass on their right side. I reached down and tried wiping a black spot with my hand. I made it worse and got black fingers for my trouble.

We gathered up the banner, trying not to drag the letters over the grass.

"We'll have to see if it will wash out," I said to Charlie.

"My mom can get these letters clean if anyone can," he offered. "My little brothers and sisters get so dirty that she undresses them beside the washing machine."

"Thanks, Charlie. Just stand the banner in a corner of the hangar for now," I said, "until we decide what to do. Then see what letters we have left for a replacement banner. I'll talk to the customer."

I knew we didn't have enough vowels to assemble the same message again. That wouldn't matter if I couldn't talk Gus Drover at the Dome into giving us another try. I walked slowly to the office. I was feeling frustrated with the banner problems and I wasn't looking forward to making the call.

"Here he is now," Summer said on the phone as I opened the door. She held out the receiver. "It's the Dome manager. He wants to talk to you."

"Hello, Gus?"

"That was brilliant!" he shouted. "I was really stupid not to realize what you had done! You have to get that banner into the air again right away! I'll pay extra, just launch it for another hour!"

His response was good news and bad news. He wasn't angry but we couldn't accommodate him.

"We don't have enough letters to make a new banner, Gus."

"No, no, no! Get the black and red one up again!"

"I don't understand. I thought you said it was unreadable."

"Forget that. People have been swarming in here," he declared excitedly. "It's the banner! The trampled look is working. They say it's so realistic that they came to see what the stampede is all about! Launch that banner now and keep it up all summer!"

Chapter Thirty

Too short

I paced off the length of ridge on the other side of the barn at home. I had decided that I could fly to work in the Super Cub if the shallow part of the rise was at least 500 feet long.

I lived in an old wooden farmhouse on ten acres of rolling pasture. My ex-wife and I had purchased the picturesque spread for two reasons: she wanted to teach English horseback riding and the place was cheap. The ridges were too steep to farm and the distance to the city was too far to commute. We moved in with the spiders, mice and their friends and then fixed up the old dairy barn for horses. I wore out several cars driving to work.

Now my wife is my ex and the horses are gone. I'm a bachelor with ten acres of hilly, hoof-pocked, horse gnawed, scrubby grass; a long commute and no place to land an airplane, except maybe a Super Cub.

A short length of ridge offered a semi-flat spot along the fence. It was the only possible place to land but it presented challenges. The prevailing wind blew from the southwest. There were power lines along the road across the southbound approach. The ridge sloped downward from there toward a creek in the middle of the property. To land into the prevailing wind I would have to fly over the wires, touch down on the ridge, let the Cub bounce down the hill, somehow cross the creek and stop by going up the ridge on the other side. The creek was big enough that I would need a bridge.

Landing to the north looked like the easier challenge. I could skim the top of the hill that crossed in front of the approach, fly nap-of-the-earth down to the creek, touch going up the next slope, brake cresting the ridge and stop before the fence at the road. It might work. The tailwind would have to be light and the ridge long enough.

On Sunday morning I practised pacing the kitchen floor tiles until I had three-foot strides. Then I walked the ridge, both ways. From the fence at the road, along the sloping ridge and partway down to the creek was 198 strides of bumpy turf, just under 600 feet. I counted 207 strides walking uphill.

Six hundred feet was plenty. The Super Cub Operating Handbook said that the stopping distance was 350 feet. That would be at maximum weight, on a level runway, flown by a test pilot in no-wind conditions. I would be lightly loaded which might make up for my less-than-perfect piloting. I rationalized that the uphill slope would compensate for the poor braking on the lumpy surface. I added 150 feet for a light tailwind. The total was 500 feet, leaving me 100 feet to spare.

I didn't worry about taking off. The book said that a fully loaded Cub needed 200 feet to depart from a standing start in no wind.

I drove to work, flew the "Dome" banner that afternoon and then practised short landings on the grass beside Runway 24. Initially I approached at 65 mph with the flaps down and some power on. Just before the chosen landing spot, I cut the power to idle, flared out and stalled the airplane onto the grass. Then I retracted the flaps, held the stick back and squeezed the heel brakes as hard as I dared to stop.

I knew from experience that the indicated stall speed with full flap was below 45 mph, the lowest number on the dial. I worked my approach speed gradually down to 50 mph indicated. I was consistently able to land and stop in less than 400 feet. I shaved a few more feet off by dropping the engine idle to 500 rpm by pulling the carburetor heat on and shutting off one side of the ignition system.

I chose the calm, cool evening on Monday for my first flight home. It felt good to be flying the commute. It helped justify the expense and effort needed to maintain an air service.

I flew over the property at 500 feet and looked down. The ridge was impossibly small. The numbers don't lie, I said to myself. Give it a try.

I started my final approach well back. The ridge looked like an anthill. I hitched myself up to see better and tightened my seat belt. I extended the flaps all the way and slowed down to 50 mph. I kept some power on, applied carb heat and shut off the left magneto. The hill in front of the ridge came up fast, too fast. I pulled the throttle back, pushed the nose down the slope and then chickened out. I initiated an overshoot: full power, carb heat off and left mag on. The Cub clawed its way up the ridge, over the fence, across the road and over the wires.

The overshoot was not as scary as the thought of not overshooting. The approach had looked too high and too fast. I could fly lower but not slower. I tried it again.

This time I flew tighter to the hill and deeper into the valley. The plane

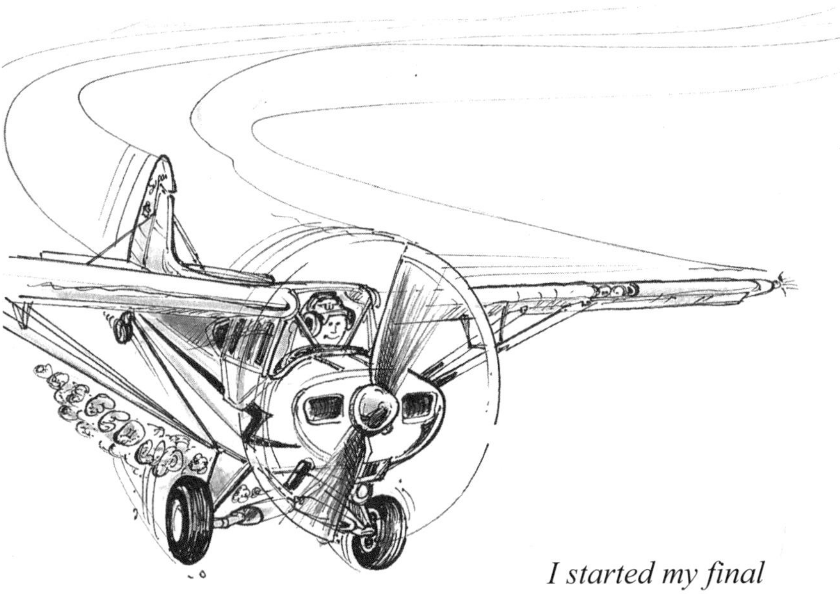

I started my final approach well back.

hung in ground effect as it crossed the creek. The oversized tires smacked the rising ridge on the other side. The Cub and I bounded back into the air and sailed over the crest of the ridge. I hit full power, shut the carb heat off and turned the second magneto on. The airplane bounced once more, hopped the far fence and then staggered over the wires.

My nap-of-the-earth flying was too high and things were happening ahead of my reactions. It was time to give it up. It wasn't worth wrecking Don's airplane to shave 20 minutes off my commute.

Then the I-can-do-anything-in-a-Super-Cub feeling took over. I was so close last time. I decided to give it one more try.

I swung the airplane around, set the flaps, speed and power, and turned on final. I focused on the hill in front of the ridge. Nearing it, I cut the power, rolled the tires onto the crest and wheeled down into the valley. I had enough speed to lever the Cub over the creek and let it three-point on the up-sloping ridge. Then I retracted the flaps and committed to a full stop.

I discovered that brakes only work when the wheels are on the ground. The fat tires repeatedly bounced off the uneven surface and locked in the air, resulting in a series of jerky hops and skids up the ridge. The fence, road and wires popped into view. They were too close and there was nothing I could do but wait for the wheels to settle onto the ground for better braking. The airplane was slowing but it was obvious that we were going to hit the low, barbed wire fence and flip into the ditch between it and the road.

I skidded the airplane to the right. It bounced down the steep side of the ridge toward the barn. I had to release the brakes so the Cub wouldn't pitch onto its nose. The next obstacle was the manure pile beside the barn. I continued turning. The Cub rocked around on the lumpy ground until it was headed back up the side of the ridge. It stopped on the incline. I let it roll back.

My eyes were wide, my heart was pounding, I was holding my breath and my bum was clamped tight. I killed the engine and sat there for a minute restarting my lungs and waiting for my pulse to stop pounding. I didn't dare relax my behind.

The silence was broken by Lady barking at the strange thing in her field. I opened the door and called her name. The barks turned to squeals. I hopped out, closed up the airplane and walked to the house.

I tried to think of why that landing was so hair-raising compared to stopping on the same distance in the airport grass.

The next morning I took off for work northbound. I was airborne in a hop, skip and a jump. Henry asked me how I made out on my first commute. I told him about the landing.

He thought for a minute. "How many nine-inch tiles did you measure in one stride?"

"Floor tiles are 12 inches," I replied.

My partner smiled and pointed to the nine-inch tiles on the office floor. "In those days they didn't make twelve-inch tiles."

Chapter Thirty-one

Rock rocks

"Circus Tower, Citabria Oscar Pop inbound." It was Rock Headley on the office monitor.

"Confirm it's Citabria Lima Oscar Oscar Papa inbound?" the controller asked.

"Affirm."

Rock didn't like saying much on the radio. "You never know who's listening," he told me.

"Oscar Oscar Papa, the active runway is 06, wind 060 at 10, altimeter 29.89; say your position, altitude and last point of departure."

"Oscar Pop at the shoreline."

"Oscar Oscar Papa, cleared to a left downwind for Runway 06, call joining, and say your last point of departure."

"Oscar Pop landing on the infield."

Rock must have departed from his "secret" fishing camp. He wasn't going to reveal its location to the controller but he might have mentioned that he was on floats.

"Oscar Oscar Papa, roger, call downwind on a left-hand approach for landing in the infield parallel and south of Runway 06, and say your last point of departure."

"Oscar Pop."

It was Tuesday and I was between flying lessons. I drove my Bug out to meet the inbound Citabria. I parked and watched the airplane line up on the infield. Rock approached nose high and power on. He flared over the burned section of grass, cut the throttle and held the airplane off as long as he could. The floats hit the short, dry grass and dug in. The airplane pitched sharply forward. It teetered on the front of the floats and almost went over before rocking back.

Rock expected the floats to slide, not dig in.

I think Rock expected the airplane to slide further and pitch less judging by the raccoon-eyed look on his face as he climbed from the cockpit.

"What happened to the long grass?" he exclaimed trying to regain his composure.

"Chainsaw Charlie trimmed it, New Brunswick style."

Rock shook his head in displeasure. "Tell the kid the next time he wants to smoke grass, I'll supply it."

"OK," I laughed. "What brings you back so soon?"

Rock jumped down from the floats and glanced into my car to see if anyone had come with me.

"I... ah... flew down for some changes on the plane," he mumbled.

"Is Darcy coming to help?" I asked.

"Not this time," he answered quietly. "I'm just touching up paint and stuff."

"Well, grab your gear and hop in. I'll give you a ride to the office."

"Thanks," he said opening the passenger door. "I don't have gear."

I drove slowly over the bumpy infield.

"I need a favour," Rock said.

"Ask away."

"The wife is bringing my van and trailer. I need to haul the plane into your hangar to take the wings off so I can tow it home," he said. "It won't take long."

It was a clear spring day. Rock could easily remove the wings outside but that was his business. There was lots of room in the hangar during the day.

"Sure, Rock, no problem."

"Thanks, pal."

"How was your first week with the airplane at your fishing camp?"

He looked at me sideways as if I knew something that I shouldn't.

I didn't.

"Fine," he replied.

"Was this the weekend Don Hitchcock fished with his buddies?"

"Yup."

"How did that go?"

"Good."

"Glad to hear it. Don has a lot of contacts. If he had fun, it could mean more business for you."

"Yeah." I could see a smirk growing on his muscled face. "Don had fun all right."

"How so?"

"Well, the group had no trouble reeling in fish all weekend; some big ones. Then I flew them one at a time back to my base. They had a good party on the shore while they waited. The game warden popped out of the bushes like a jack-in-the-box when I was returned with the last of their gear. Apparently he had been waiting to nab us.

The guy looked pretty silly jumping out of the sumac in his uniform and pointing his finger at us like a gun. Don started to laugh. He laughed harder when the warden pulled the stringers of over-catch from the stream. He roared when we were being lectured. The warden got really upset. Then I thought Don would die laughing when the guy confiscated the fish, all the fishing gear and my airplane."

"Wholly smoke!" I exclaimed.

Rock grinned. "I asked Don later why he thought it was so funny. The crazy bugger said he liked drinking with his buddies in the wilderness but he sure didn't want to clean and eat the fish."

"How did you get the airplane back?"

"Don," Rock replied. "He did it in one day. He talked to the Minister of Soil and Sea who was about to benefit from a government supported development in his riding. I got to keep my airplane but that made the game warden mad. He's going to be all over me now. That's why I want to make some cosmetic changes on the bird."

"That's good. I mean... it's good you got the Citabria back."

"Yeah," Rock chuckled, "especially since it's still 90 per cent Don's airplane."

Chapter Thirty-two

Banner super sales

The manager of the Niagara Falls Dome signed a contract for a two-hour banner tow from one to three o'clock every Saturday, Sunday and holiday through to the fall. I felt like our aerial advertising business was finally taking off.

Don Hitchcock launched his re-election campaign with a banner advertisement. His abbreviation for "Conservative Party" caught a lot of attention. The Niagara Falls Cataract newspaper ran a picture of the Cub towing his banner over the city.

"RE-ELECT HITCHCOCK-CON PARTY"

We traded Don aerial advertising for our lease payments on his Super Cub. His business didn't add to our cash flow but his comical message made our telephone ring.

I spent Wednesday in Niagara Falls following up customer leads generated by Hitchcock's banner. I came back with zero contracts. It was the same problem at each stop. Every business wanted the early afternoon time slot on the weekends. It was discouraging to think that we had maxed out the banner revenue at four hours per week. So much for my money-making idea.

Chainsaw Charlie dropped by the airport on Wednesday evening when I was closing up. I was pushing a Cherokee into the hangar on my own.

"Hi there big guy, what's up?"

"Hi, sir. I wanted to speak to you. Can I give you a hand?"

"Absolutely."

I was leaning my weight on the tow bar. The kid pushed on the wing root. I stumbled forward as the airplane shot toward the hangar.

"Not so hard, Charlie!"

"Sorry."

"That's OK. What do you want to talk about?"

He spoke slowly. "I was thinking if we had more banner business I'd get more hours making the messages and setting them up."

"We both want the same thing, Charlie. I spent all of today in Niagara Falls and didn't land one contract."

He paused to think about that one. "I was wondering if you'd let me sell some banner towing?"

"Gee, Charlie... I don't know."

It bothered me to think of the 14-year-old driving illegally in his mother's pick-up trying to sell our aerial ad service. I scrambled to think of a way to turn him down.

He looked at his feet and then at me. "Well, I... ah... know some different people who might be interested."

"Charlie, what does your mom think about it?"

I figured teenagers acted first and asked their parents last. I was counting on my question slowing him down.

"She says it's fine if it doesn't interfere with my school work and if I'm not just driving around."

The youngster was ahead of me.

"See, that's just it, Charlie. I drove around Niagara Falls for nothing."

"If you let me try selling for a week," he persisted, "it won't cost you anything. I'll pay for the gas in the truck and do it on my own time."

The determined look on the kid's face told me to say, Yes. He had always worked hard and had never let us down.

"Well, Charlie, I suppose it can't hurt."

A big grin flashed across his face. "Thanks boss, you won't be sorry."

"That's good but here's the deal. You pay your expenses and sell on your own time, like you said. We'll pay you a ten per cent commission on the advertising you sell. That'll be separate from what you earn assembling banners and setting them up."

I knew that selling aerial advertising was wishful thinking for the Grade 8 student but I wanted him to think I was taking his offer seriously. Charlie dressed in a worn checked shirt and green work pants. His face was always covered in heavy dark stubble. The way he looked, the only thing people would buy from him was firewood.

"You don't have to pay me a commission," he said. "I'd be happy working the extra hours at the airport."

"No, that's the deal, take it or leave it."

I held out my hand. He shook it.

"It's a deal," he said.

"Thatta boy!" I was going to slap him on the shoulder but stopped myself. I didn't want him to slap me back. I turned. "Come on into the office and I'll fix you up with some advertising brochures."

"I got them already," he answered quietly.

"Well, you seem to know what you're doing. You might take one of the better letters from the rack to show to the customers."

He looked at his feet. "I've got one in the truck."

"Well, I guess you're all set."

He looked up and smiled. "Yes, sir."

Charlie didn't need a week to sell aerial advertising. After school on Thursday he landed two contracts. The first was for one hour, from four to five o'clock, on Saturday afternoons for the whole summer. The Circus Speedway had a problem and Charlie solved it. They ran stock car races on the dirt track every Saturday evening when the weather was good. The problem was letting the public know each week if the races were on or weathered out. Charlie's solution was a late afternoon banner tow when the races were on.

He drove to the airport to tell us about it.

"The Speedway is my mom's favourite," he explained. "Kids under 12 get in free and she has seven of them. We bundle them up, take them to the track and fill them with foot-long hotdogs. My brothers and sisters love it. They get to stay up late and they can yell and scream all they want. No one can hear them when the cars are running."

Charlie said that his family was well known to the track owners. He suggested to them that the weekly banner tow would signal that the races were on as well as bring in new customers. They bought it.

The banner was to be the same each week; "CAR WARS-7PM-CIRCUS SPDWAY".

The second contract was with Bigmouth Pizza, a local chain.

"They have Tightwad Tuesdays," Charlie said. "Order a pizza on Tuesdays and get a second same-size pizza for free. Mom gets two party squares. It's the best deal on enough food to feed all of us."

"I've seen the Bigmouth ads on the public benches at the bus stops."

"Yeah. I told the owner that one big lady with groceries can wipe out a whole bench ad. I said that the banner is always visible to everyone outside and we can tow it anywhere. He signed up for an hour every Tuesday for the rest of the year."

"What message does he want us to tow?"

"2FOR1 PIZZA-DIAL BIG-MOUT-H"

"That's great, Charlie!"

"Next week I'm going to visit our grocer, dentist and discount store."

Chapter Thirty-three

Cornfield stakeout

Friday was my morning to sleep in. A knock at the door followed by Lady's bark woke me up at 6:30. I was in my bachelor pajamas, the clothes from the night before, so I rolled out of bed and went down the stairs.

Jan Vandenstock, a neighbouring dairy farmer, was standing on the side porch. I opened the door.

"Jan, come in. What brings you here so early?"

The older Dutchman shuffled through the door. The smell of cow barn followed him.

He smiled shyly. "Dis not so early vhen you milk at four turdy," he said. "I vaited so I don't vake you too much."

"No problem, Jan. It was time for me to get up anyway. What can I do for you?"

"I tought you should know dat visitors come de last two days." He paused while Lady vacuumed his pants with her nose, up one leg and down the other.

I said nothing. I had learned that Jan was better at talking to cows than neighbours. I let him gather his words.

"Vednesday mornink, car drive into corn field by de road. Two men, dey sit in lawn chairs vid binoculars." He swallowed and looked around the kitchen. His eyes settled on the pile of dishes in the sink.

"That sounds strange," I offered.

"Dey dere all day. Afternoon milkink time, dey fold up chairs and leave."

Jan was the kind of neighbour who kept to himself. He'd give you the shirt off his back if you needed it but you didn't see him much until you did. I had no idea how his story qualified for one of his rare visits.

"Tursday dey back at nine o'clock," he continued. "Same sit by corn field vid binoculars. Before next milkink, I go talk to dem. Dey ask about airplane coming to secret landing. I don't understand but I remember you flyink around Monday night."

I could smell trouble brewing, for me.

"I say to dem, a neighbour fly home in little plane sometime. Dey vant to know many tings about you and plane dat I don't know."

"Yes, Jan, and what did you say?"

He imitated the shrug he always gave when he was done talking. "I say to ask you demselves. Den I tell dem it might take long time. You fly home vonce in five years."

I wanted to burst out laughing but I didn't.

"Were these guys young: one heavy and the other slim?" I asked.

"Ya."

"Were they dressed up?"

"Ya."

"Was their car a dark blue colour?"

"Ya. Dese are friends lookink for you?"

"Not exactly, but I have met them before. I don't think they will be back today."

Jan shrugged and turned toward the door. "Too bad. I could put dem to vork."

I smiled. "Thanks for letting me know."

"You velcome."

Chapter Thirty-four

Stealth on floats

"I have two messages for you," Leanne said, when I arrived at the office later Friday morning.

"Shoot."

"Rock Headley called for you. He wanted to fit the wings on his float-plane in our hangar. I told him it was OK."

"Good. When is he coming?"

"He's here now. He said that it won't take long."

I smiled. "That sounds like Rock."

"And Melville booked a banner flight for this Sunday evening."

"Melville Passmore?"

"Yes," she smiled. "The newly-weds are back from their honeymoon and apparently still in love."

"Why do you say it like that?"

"The message he wants is 'HAPPY BIRTHDAY MARY ELLEN'. It's his wife's birthday on Sunday. Melville is taking her out for supper at the Shoreline Restaurant." Our receptionist was getting starry-eyed as she spoke. "Isn't that romantic?"

"It would be except his wife's name is Betty-Lou," I joked.

Leanne's head snapped down. She quickly scanned her message book. "No, it's not!" she declared.

"I'm just kidding," I said, "but it makes me think there is another untapped source of banner business."

"Oh, good luck!" she exclaimed sarcastically. "Other men don't do things like that."

"Are you referring to any Henry in particular?"

"Now you're spoiling it for me."

"Would it be better if I told you that Melville's wife is deaf. A banner message would be the perfect birthday gift."

"Ohhhhhh! That's soooo wonderful!"

I left Leanne to swoon and walked out to the hangar. Rock and his wife were attaching a wing to a fuselage. I didn't recognize the airplane.

"Hi, Rock. Hi, Sandy. Where did this come from?"

Rock was standing on a pontoon torquing the bolts at the wing roots. His petite wife was holding onto a yellow rope that ran to a pulley in the rafters and down to the middle of the wing. I expected her to be yanked to the ceiling any second.

"From my place," Rock replied. "I didn't think you'd mind if I put the wings on in the hangar. It won't take long."

"No problem," I replied. "Sandy, do you need help on that rope?"

"I'm fine," she grimaced.

"You must have lead in your boots."

"Don't give Rocko any more ideas."

I looked closely at the airplane. The shape was Citabria but the paint colour was battleship grey. "Is this your Citabria, Rock?"

"Yup. I painted it. What do you think?"

The paint was thick and uneven on the fabric covering. In places, red stars were faintly visible from underneath. Only the windows and tires had escaped the rough-looking coating.

"Well, it's grey."

"Yeah. I tried spraying it but it would have taken forever to cover the starbursts so I rollered it."

"I see that, but why paint it at all?"

"Camouflage," Rock replied. He jumped off the float to the trailer. "Hang on, honey," he said to his wife. "We just have to fit the struts and then we're done this side." He looked at me. "Can you help me with the struts? It'll only take a minute."

"Sure."

I held the "V" strut in place while Rock lined up the bolts under the wing.

"So is this supposed to make you invisible to game wardens?"

"It'll make me harder to spot," he replied.

"Wouldn't it be easier to obey the fish and game laws?"

"Oh, I'll be doing that for sure," he laughed. He moved down to where the struts attached to the fuselage. "In the meantime, one game warden in particular wants to harass me out of business." He paused. "A little higher, honey."

Sandy pulled on the rope.

"More. Whoa. Hold it there." He slid a bolt into place. "He'll want to check all of my customers' gear and licences going in and their catch coming out. He'll use a micrometer to measure fish length. He'll pin something on me sooner or later but he has to find me first. I've got a new jumping off place where he'll never think to look. The paint job will make it hard for him to see me in the air."

"Well, good luck. If you're OK for now, I'll go flying with my first student."

"Maybe you and your student would like to help with the other wing?" Rock suggested. "It won't take long."

"No thanks. I make more money flying with him," I replied, "if you don't mind."

"No, not at all."

The other wing was on the Citabria when I taxied in with my first student. After my second lesson, the trailer was out of the hangar and the floatplane looked ready to go. I gave Rock a thumbs-up as I walked to the office. He waved me over.

"Say, when you're done with your student, can you help us take this thing off the trailer in the infield? I want to do it like Darcy showed us last week."

"Sure Rock. I'll be with you in a couple of minutes."

"I knew I could count on you," he said, slapping me on the shoulder. "It won't take long."

Sandy and I each held a rope tied to one of the Citabria's floats. Rock jerked the trailer from underneath the airplane with his van. Sandy managed to dig in her cowgirl boots. I was yanked off my feet.

"Are you OK?" Sandy asked.

"Oh, yeah. It's nothing that I haven't experienced before," I replied, looking at the new rope burns on my hands.

The airport maintenance truck headed our way when Rock laid two barrels of used oil on their sides at the back of the trailer. Their spigots were hanging over the edge. He was going to open them and drive ahead leaving parallel slippery trails for his takeoff.

The truck stopped and Barney Swallow charged out. He pointed at me.

"What in tarnation do you think you're doing?"

Before I could answer, Rock walked over to him grinning. "Hi, I'm Rock Headley," he said, offering a handshake. "He's helping me get this floatplane launched."

Barney ignored the hand. "Not that way, he's not," the airport manager declared. He pointed to the oil barrels.

"Whatever you say, sir. We meant no harm. It's too bad, though. I've got three guys waiting for me to fly them to a remote fishing lake."

Barney's old eyes narrowed. Then they focused on Rock. "What kind of fish?"

"Pickerel," Rock replied. "It's too early for bass."

"There's no good pickerel fishing around here," Barney declared.

"There is where I go."

Barney rubbed his face thoughtfully with both hands. "Just wait a minute," he said.

He retreated to his truck. I could see him talking on the radio. He returned and spoke to Rock. "We'll get you off shortly but not that way," he said, nodding toward the oil drums. "You'll have to move your van and trailer off to one side."

Rock obliged.

I could hear fire engine sirens in the distance. They grew louder. Two familiar fire trucks, one pumper and one tanker, roared across the ramp and bumped over the infield toward us. They stopped and six firemen jumped out, three from each truck.

The round fire chief hustled toward us as fast as he could. His big boots and coat flapped with each step. It was the same older guy I had met at Charlie's grass fire. The other firemen unrolled hose behind him.

"Where's the fire?" he bellowed as he approached Barney.

"No fire," the airport manager replied.

"Then what's the callout for?"

"We need your men to hose the grass so this airplane can take off," Barney answered calmly.

The stubby fireman planted his gauntlets on his hips. "You stupid old fool! You called in a fire alarm to get your lawn watered?"

"That's right." Barney's craggy face twisted into a smirk. "I hear your guys need the practice."

"If that don't beat all!" The chief stamped his feet in frustration. "Barney, you can't summon municipal emergency services for something like that!"

"Well, since you're here and the hoses are out, how about giving us a squirt?"

The red-faced chief turned and motioned for his men to stop setting up.

"It's the only way we can get this guy going," Barney called after him. "He's flying friends into a lake where the pickerel are as big as carp!"

The chief stopped and turned around. "There's no good pickerel fishing around here," he declared.

"There is where he's going."

"Where's that?"

"First the grass gets wet, then we talk about a fly-in fishing trip." Barney turned to Rock. "Right son?"

"Yes sirree," Rock replied.

Rock was off and running as soon as we started the Citabria moving.

The fire brigade hosed the grass in front of the floatplane. It was a good thing they stayed for the takeoff. Rock ran the Citabria's engine to full power and rocked it back and forth but it wouldn't slide on the wet grass. I motioned for the firemen to push on the floats. That did the trick. Rock was off and running as soon as we started him moving. He lifted off and turned northbound.

Sandy gave me a ride back to the office. Summer McDay was there sewing letters and Leanne was just leaving for the day.

"I was thinking," Leanne said, "it would be really nice if we went to the Shoreline Restaurant for supper Sunday and surprised Melville, after the banner flight, of course. Summer said that she'd go. How about you?"

"What did Henry say about it?"

Leanne's face reddened. "I'm asking you first. If you'll go, so will he, and then I can too."

"Who's flying the banner?"

Her face turned redder. "Oh, I forgot. Someone has to tow the banner and it's your day off. I guess Henry will be there but he'll be flying by in the Super Cub."

"Well, I'm coming in to tow the advertisement for the Dome since Henry is booked up with flying lessons all afternoon. I'll stay to do Melville's message if you can talk your husband into taking you out to dinner."

"I'll work on it."

I discovered Rock's new fishing jump-off point later that day. My next booking was to fly the Super Cub to Toronto to pick up Don Hitchcock from a political meeting. The lakefront airport in the heart of the big city's downtown also had floatplane facilities.

I landed and headed for the ramp. On the way I taxied past a stealth-coloured Citabria bobbing at the seaplane dock. Office towers loomed in the background. Rock was loading gear into the back of the airplane.

Don was waiting for me at the old wooden terminal building.

"Did you see my bush pilot at the seaplane dock?" Don asked.

"Yeah. Did you see the paint job he laid on your former airplane?"

"The grey submarine?" Don chuckled. "That kid sure is determined. Flying to remote lakes from here should keep him out of trouble for now."

"Why do you say that?"

"How many fish and game wardens are there in downtown Toronto?"

Chapter Thirty-five

"This is cool."

I telephoned Ray Tragunno on Saturday morning. Ray had instructed with Henry and me at another flying school. Now he was a second officer at Major Airlines flying sideways in the flight engineer's seat of an early model Boeing 747. Ray had done some part-time instructing for us when Henry and I had started The Flying Circus. These days he'd drop by when the weather was bad. He liked shooting the breeze in our lounge and drinking our bad coffee. He said it allowed him to relive his instructing days without actually going back to them.

"Hi, Ray. I've got a proposition for you."

"The last time you said that my wife found out I was flying with nubile college students. It cost me a mink coat and a lot of promises that I won't talk about. I can't afford another hit like that."

"This is different Ray: no instructing, no passengers either; just flying nowhere on your own."

"I'm listening."

"We need help towing banners with the Super Cub."

"I'm not interested."

"Wait a minute. We pay double the instructing rate."

Ray laughed. "The airline pays ten times your rate and I spend overnights away from home in nice hotels with pretty cabin crews."

"But this is low flying, Ray."

"So."

"You can see everything: swimming pools, nudist camps, beaches and neighbourhood backyards."

"And I just fly around?"

"Right. And only in good weather. With the banner on, the Cub practically flies itself."

"I don't know. I'm pretty busy."

"How about one afternoon a week?"

"This month I fly to Europe Mondays and back on Wednesdays. I baby-sit Thursdays and Fridays while Helga works and Saturday when she takes the day off from the family. The only afternoon left is Sunday."

"That's perfect. Drop by tomorrow by three and I'll check you out."

Ray fit the image of an airline pilot. He was tall and good looking. He had a deep voice that made him sound older than he was.

On Sunday he was too tall for the Super Cub. He squeezed into the front seat after much grunting and creative language. He sat with his legs jammed under the instrument panel and his head tilted to avoid the ceiling crossbar. He looked like he was flying a kiddy ride. He had limited movement of the control stick and couldn't push the rudder pedals at all.

"I thought William Piper was a big man," Ray said in frustration.

"He was but he didn't fly."

"Now I see why."

"I have an idea. If you can get out, I'll remove the seat cushion and that'll give you a few more inches."

Ray contorted himself out of the Cub. I unsnapped the plastic pilot seat revealing the steel frame. He stuffed himself back in. Now he could hold his head up and move his legs a little. He tried the controls.

"It should work," he said. "If I need extra rudder pedal I'll reach for the ones in the back."

"Well, we'll give it a try."

Ray was so big I couldn't climb into the rear seat with him already in the front.

"I'm sorry Ray, but I have to ask you to climb out again and let me get in first."

"I don't believe this. There's more room in a 747 washroom than in this airplane."

"Think of it as an evacuation exercise."

Ray wormed his way out. I climbed into the back seat. Ray refolded himself into the front. I looked forward. All that I could see was Ray. About 120 degrees of my forward vision was blocked by the big guy. I could see so little there was no reason for me to go on this flight but I didn't want to ask him to climb out again. I shut up and went along for the ride.

Ray took off with the door open and the cable and hook in his lap. The slipstream blasted through the door and pounded me in the face and chest. Now I couldn't see or hear. Ray tossed out the cable on the downwind leg and closed the door.

Chainsaw Charlie had made up a short banner for us to advertise our flying school.

"LEARN TO FLY HERE"

Ray descended and turned final. I could only assume that he was lined up with the pick-up poles. He added power to level off. I looked out the side. We were impossibly high.

"Lower, Ray."

"I'm too low already!"

"No, you're not. Drop down."

He shaved off a few feet from our altitude. We went sailing over the pick-up loop about 200 feet too high. Ray hit full power and zoomed into a climb. We passed by Chainsaw. He was standing next to his pick-up truck holding his arms up in a "What gives?" gesture.

"Try it again, Ray, lower, much lower."

On his next pass, he was still too high.

"Lower!" I shouted.

"If we were in the 747, the wheels would be on the ground!" he exclaimed.

We missed the loop.

"Ray, you know how they teach you to land the 747 by looking well ahead?"

"Yeah."

"Don't do that here. Focus on Charlie's pick-up truck."

"OK."

Ray hooked the rope on the next pass, with some help. He was lower as we approached the poles but still too high. I looked down on the left side when he hit full power. I could see Charlie below. He was standing on his tiptoes and holding the loop as high in the air as he could with the left pole.

The big airline pilot zoomed into a climb and leveled off. The airplane plowed along. We were gaining height but only by inches.

It was the warmest day of the spring. I had noticed the Cub's reduced performance while towing the "Dome" banner earlier in the afternoon but I didn't appreciate how heavy Ray had become since joining the airlines. The Cub was acting like it was towing a full-sized banner with the old pitch on the propeller.

"Seventy miles per hour Ray?"

"You got it."

I pushed on my copy of the throttle. It was wide open.

"Carb heat off, Ray?"

"Check."

"Mags on Both?"

"Check."

"Turn left and look out the window to see if the banner is twisted."

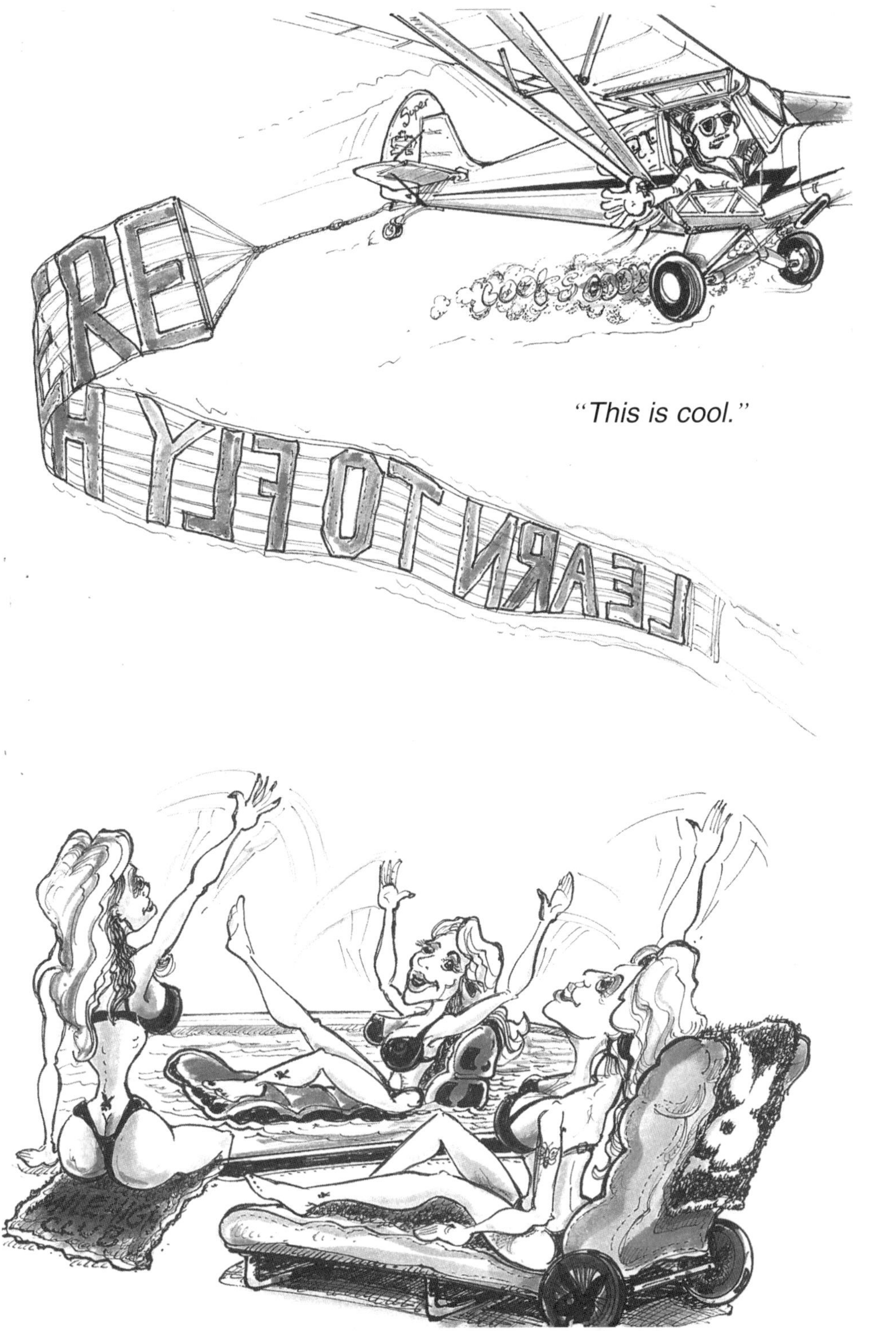

"This is cool."

Ray banked the airplane. We lost height. He glanced backward. "Looks good."

That meant that the only way we could climb was to burn off fuel.

"Better avoid the built-up areas until we gain more altitude," I said.

Ray nodded. He was looking down and smiling. I followed his gaze. There was a big new country house about 300 feet below with a swimming pool behind it. Three girls were lounging beside the pool in bathing suits. Ray stuck an arm out the window and waved. They waved back.

"Hey, you're right," Ray enthused. "This is cool. I can see everything from here."

That was it. Ray was hooked on banner towing.

"I'm glad your eyes are enjoying it. By the way, do you have time to tow a revenue banner along the shoreline for me?"

"When?"

"Now."

"Sure."

"Good. Let's head back to the airport. I'll show you how to release this banner and help you set up the next one."

Ray and I didn't have to descend much to fly our low pass. We dropped the message beside the birthday banner for Melville's wife that Chainsaw had already laid out.

Thirty minutes later, Ray hooked the rope on his first try. He approached too high but this time Chainsaw and I each held up a pole as high as we could. It was enough.

Chapter Thirty-six

Surprise

I jumped into my Volkswagen and raced to the restaurant. I was going so fast that I was almost keeping up with the traffic. I turned into the Shoreline Restaurant's driveway in time to see the Super Cub flying low along the waterfront. The early evening sun was behind the banner making the big letters glow. It looked great.

There was a group of people standing in the restaurant parking lot waving at the airplane. Ray stuck an arm out and waved back. The gathering looked too big to be from the airport. Then I recognized Leanne and Henry, then Summer and her brother Barry. I parked and walked toward them. Darcy was there with his wife Mimi. I saw Melville's parents next to Mary Ellen's parents and their daughter Portia. Al Milton was also in the group along with a few other customers who knew Melville.

As I got closer, I saw Barney Swallow with a woman who must have been his wife. "Barney, I'm surprised to see you at an airport function," I teased. "Isn't this your day off?"

"Leanne invited me," he replied in his gravely voice. "She said you were paying for supper so I brought my wife." He clicked his dentures. "This is Jean."

"Pleased to meet you," we said at the same time and then laughed.

Behind Barney was Ziggy Burns standing beside a blond woman. She was younger, taller, better looking and much better dressed than the tough little instructor.

"Leanne invited us too," Ziggy said. "This is my wife, Bubbles. We came since you're paying."

Bubbles smiled and revealed a wad of chewing gum. "Pleathed to meet youthe," she said.

Don Hitchcock drove into the parking lot in his big Buick. He rolled

*All that I got
was forehead.*

out of the driver's seat. "Looks like we're in time, Honey," he said, turning to a woman getting out of the other side. "Come on, I want you to meet some people."

He caught my eye and marched right over. He grabbed my shoulder and motioned to the woman walking our way. "Honey, this is my pilot. He's the one who brings me home to you every Friday." He turned to me. "This is my current wife, Honey. All my wives are Honey. It's easier to keep them straight that way. Thanks for buying supper. I never miss a free chance to campaign for my re-election." He grabbed the hand of the person next to me. "Hi, my name is Don Hitchcock. I'm your faithful political representative..."

I noticed Carol Thomas standing at the back of the group. She was watching the birthday banner continue down the coast. I moved toward her, greeting the rest of the gathering on the way. Carol looked better than ever. She was nicely dressed and her face was set in a shy, dreamy look that suited her well.

"Hi, Carol."

She turned her head toward me and smiled.

"Hello."

"Did Leanne invite you to join us?" I asked quickly. "I meant to call but we've been so busy. Every time I remembered, I was never near a phone." I stopped. I was sounding lame.

She stepped closer and looked up at me. "Actually, it was Summer McDay who called and suggested that I come tonight," she said. "I'm glad she did. The banner was a wonderfully romantic thing that Melville did for Mary Ellen's birthday."

That explained the dreamy look.

Carol then slid her arms around my waist, rested her head on my shoulder and hugged me. It was the last thing that I expected from this confident but reserved schoolteacher. It was out of character for the country girl who I thought I knew, but I was the one blushing.

She lifted her head off my shoulder and looked at me with big eyes. "Oh, I didn't mean to embarrass you," she said. "You looked like you needed a hug. I did too so I helped myself."

She let go of me. I replied by putting my arms around her and bending down to give her a kiss. All that I got was forehead. She stepped back.

"Maybe we should join the others," she said.

I turned. The parking lot was empty except for the cars and us.

Inside, the surprise had been sprung on the newlyweds. Everyone was milling around their table. Melville was standing and pumping hands vigorously.

"Oh, my gosh," he declared several times. "How did you know we were here?"

Mary Ellen sat with her hands in her lap. She was reading lips and thanking each person as they wished her a Happy Birthday.

Leanne had arranged for a long table to be set up next to the couple. Carol and I sat down with the group. Drinks were ordered and served, followed by our meals. Easy laughter carried up and down the table. Many of the jokes were about me.

"You should have seen him dragging that oversized banner to Niagara Falls," Barry McDay said. "I thought for sure he'd snag someone's clothesline with it!"

"I told him not to fly a banner that long," Ziggy added.

"That's the one he dropped on the elephants!" Al Milton roared.

It was all in good fun but Carol was hearing it for the first time. The stories had to be inflating my bumbling reputation in her eyes. She was smiling at the laughter. I wished that we could be alone.

She looked at me. "Your friends must really like you," she said, "to tell these stories in front to you."

But why do they have to tell them in front of you? I asked myself.

Someone shouted and pointed at the windows. "Look!"

We turned to see the Super Cub flying from right to left, low and in tight to the restaurant. We could see Ray Tragunno in the pilot's seat. It was obvious that he was laughing. A towrope was attached to the airplane's tail followed by a banner. We read it as each word came into view.

"HONEY, WE'RE PREGNANT"

I looked at Leanne sitting halfway down the table to see what she knew. She looked at me in surprise. I shrugged. She shrugged back. Ray must have cooked this one up with Chainsaw.

In the meantime, Henry was staring at Leanne with his mouth open.

Don Hitchcock turned to his wife. "Honey, say it isn't so!"

"Not another one!" Darcy exclaimed to Mimi.

Ziggy frowned at Bubbles. She shrugged and continued eating.

Melville's parents vigorously shook their heads back and forth.

Then the laughter started.

"Boy, that really got everyone going," Al Milton chuckled.

"The whole city will see that," Barry said. "I wouldn't want to be answering the telephone in the control tower tonight."

Summer spoke next. "Or in the office at The Flying Circus."

Henry called down the table to me. "What do you know about this?"

"Nothing, Henry, I swear, but you know Ray. If you were him, you'd fly laughing too."

About the Author

Garth Wallace is from St. Catharines, Ontario, near Niagara Falls, where he learned to fly in a Fleet Canuck in 1966. From 1971 until 1990, Garth worked full time at various locations as a flying instructor, bush pilot and corporate pilot. It was during those flying years that he met the colourful characters and lived the humorous experiences that are the basis for his seven-book series of funny flying stories. Garth now lives near Ottawa, Ontario, Canada with his wife Liz.

About the Artist

Francois Bougie's interest in aviation was sparked at an early age by his father who restored several aircraft and constructed two homebuilts. Francois' passion led to a college education as an aircraft maintenance engineer and a career as an electromechanical designer in the aerospace industry in Montreal, Quebec. In the 1990s, Francois began applying an artistic talent to aviation art and industrial technical illustrations. His work has been published on several aviation book covers, posters and in aviation magazines. Francois is a licenced pilot. He has owned a Cessna 120 and a Pitts Special. He currently flies a classic 1946 Globe Swift that he restored.

Other books by Garth Wallace

You'd Fly Laughing Too is the seventh book in a series of funny flying stories written by Garth Wallace. Here is more information on previous funny tales plus other aviation humour books published by Happy Landings.
Ordering information appears on page 200.

Fly Yellow Side Up

The hilarious story of a suburban pilot who moves north seeking the freedom and glory of flying floatplanes. Follow Wallace as he takes a bush pilot job with no floatplane experience and stumbles his way into the fascinating world of wilderness flying.

Soft cover

Pie In The Sky

Laugh with Wallace as he learns that the riches to be found running a small-town flying school are not in the money but in the characters and the memories. In ***Pie In The Sky*** *Wallace discovers cowboy agricultural pilots, Mennonite buggy buzzing and other off-the-wall aviation adventures.*

Soft cover

Cockpit Follies

Student pilot Marathon Melville, aircraft salesman Skid Sicamore and a parking lot vigilante named "The Snitch" are some of the crazy characters in this hilarious book by Canada's leading aviation humorist, Garth Wallace.

Soft cover

The Flying Circus

Get ready to laugh again as Happy Landings presents more funny flying stories by Garth Wallace. ***The Flying Circus*** *is a humourous tale of two instructors who start a flying school with loads of enthusiasm, little business sense and no money.*

Soft cover

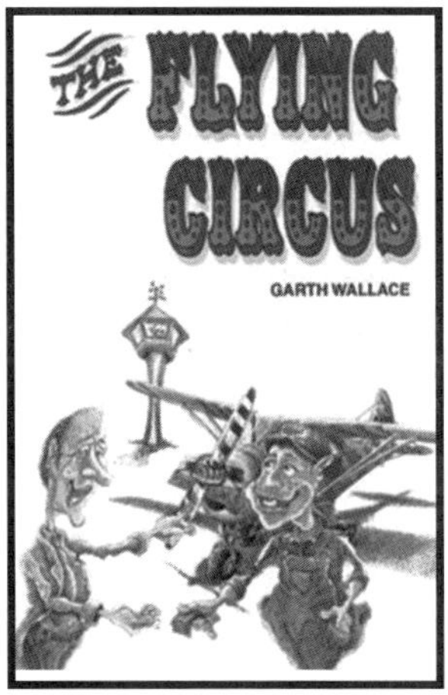

If Clouds Could Talk

The humour shifts to corporate aviation. Ride with Wallace as he flies eye-to-eye past the Statue of Liberty, radios a rhyming radar operator and learns aerobatic flying from a sadistic mortician.

Soft cover

An aviation biography by Garth Wallace

Don't Call Me a Legend

This is a true adventure story about a modern-day Canadian aviation legend. The inspiring biography follows Charlie Vaughn as he works his way from sky-gazing farm boy to a world renowned ferry pilot. Fly with Charlie as he delivers a Cessna Skymaster to Botswana, a Twin Otter across the Pacific, a Hawker Siddeley through Russia and many other global adventures. *Hard cover*

Other books published by Happy Landings

Papa X-Ray - Jim Lang

Papa X-Ray is the true story of a trusty old airplane, a family adjusting to life in the far north and a greenhorn pilot learning to fly in the spectacular ruggedness of Canada's Northwest Territories. Follow Jim Lang as he trades a trailer for an airplane and flies it as family transportation through the wilderness around Nahanni Butte. *Soft cover*

Ace McCool - Jack Desmarais

Ace McCool spoofs the airline industry through the laughter-packed exploits of Down East International, a fictional "fly-by-night" operation based in Moncton, New Brunswick. These tall tales brought laughter to thousands of aviators reading Canadian Aviation magazine. Now, they have been assembled in a collector edition book. *Soft cover*

Magnetic North - *David Halsey*

Magnetic North *chronicles a coast-to-coast trek across northern Canada by foot, dogsled and canoe. What started as the Trans-Canada Expedition became a gripping adventure for two young men who set out to rediscover the Canadian North the hard way.* *Hard cover*